1st Workshop on Semantics-Driven Statistical Machine Translation 2015

AA005639

Co-located with ACL-IJCNLP 2015

Beijing, China
30 July 2015

Editors:

Deyi Xiong
Kevin Duh
Christian Hardmeier
Roberto Navigli

ISBN: 978-1-5108-0945-1

Printed from e-media with permission by:

Curran Associates, Inc.
57 Morehouse Lane
Red Hook, NY 12571

Some format issues inherent in the e-media version may also appear in this print version.

Printed by Curran Associates, Inc. (2015)

Association for Computational Linguistics
209 N. Eighth Street
Stroudsburg, Pennsylvania 18360

Phone: 1-570-476-8006
Fax: 1-570-476-0860

acl@aclweb.org

Additional copies of this publication are available from:

Curran Associates, Inc.
57 Morehouse Lane
Red Hook, NY 12571 USA
Phone: 845-758-0400
Fax: 845-758-2634
Email: curran@proceedings.com
Web: www.proceedings.com

Proceedings of S^2MT 2015

The 1st Workshop on Semantics-Driven Statistical Machine Translation

Deyi Xiong, Kevin Duh,
Christian Hardmeier and Roberto Navigli (editors)

ACL-IJCNLP 2015 Workshop
July 30, 2015
Beijing, China

Preface

We are very pleased to welcome you to the 1st Workshop on Semantics-Driven Statistical Machine Translation (S^2MT) in conjunction with ACL, held on July 30, 2015 at Beijing, China.

Over the last two decades, statistical machine translation (SMT) has made a substantial progress from word-based to phrase and syntax-based SMT. Recently the progress curve has reached a stage where translation quality increases more slowly even if we use sophisticated syntactic forest-based models for translation. On the other hand, crucial meaning errors, such as incorrect translations of word senses and semantic roles, are still pervasive in SMT-generated translation hypotheses. These errors sometimes make the meanings of target translations significantly drift from the original meanings of source sentences. With an eye on the current dilemma of SMT, one might ask questions: Does SMT reach the maturity stage of its lifespan? Or is it time for us to find a new direction for SMT in order to catalyse next breakthroughs?

Semantics-driven SMT may be one of these breaking points. Semantics at different levels may enable SMT to generate not only grammatical but also meaning-preserving translations. Lexical semantics provides useful information for sense and semantic role disambiguation during translation. Compositional semantics allows SMT to generate target phrase and sentence translations by means of semantic composition. Discourse semantics captures inter-sentence dependencies for document-level machine translation. Large-scale semantic knowledge bases such as WordNet, YAGO and BabelNet, can provide external semantic knowledge for SMT. Semantics-driven SMT allows us to gradually shift from syntax to semantics and offers insights on how meaning is correctly conveyed during translation.

The goals of this workshop are to identify key challenges of exploring semantics in SMT, to discuss how semantics can help SMT and how SMT can benefit from rapid developments of semantic technologies theoretically and practically, and to find new opportunities emerging from the combination of semantics and SMT. Our key interest is to provide insights into semantics-driven SMT. Specifically, the motivations of this workshop are:

- To bring researchers in the SMT and semantics community together and to cultivate new ideas for cutting-edge models and algorithms of semantic SMT.
- To theoretically examine what semantics can provide for SMT and how SMT can benefit from semantics from a broad perspective.
- To explore new research horizons for semantics-driven SMT in practice.

We received 8 submissions from Asia, Europe and USA. After a rigorous selection, we only accepted 4 high-quality papers in the workshop program. The accepted papers examine and explore semantics in machine translation from different angles and perspectives. Alastair Butler studies the round-trip transformations between parsed sentences and meaning representations. Elior Sulem, Omri Abend and Ari Rappoport investigate semantic annotations in contrast to syntactic annotations using French-English language pair as a case study. Jinan Xu, Jiangming Liu, Yufeng Chen, Yujie Zhang, Fang Ming and Shaotong Li incorporate case frames into hierarchical phrase-based Japanese-Chinese translation. Aleš Tamchyna, Chris Quirk and Michel Galley present an abstract meaning representation to string translation model in a discriminative framework.

In addition to the accepted papers, we are very delighted to invite 4 distinguished keynote speakers from semantics and machine translation to cover topics that cross boundaries of these two areas. Percy Liang (Stanford University) and Gerard de Melo (Tsinghua University) will give talks in the morning session, which connect semantic parsing and multilingual semantics to machine translation. Quoc V. Le (Google) will give a talk on neural language understanding in the afternoon session. Finally, António Branco (University of Lisbon) will present high-quality translation via deep language engineering approaches.

The workshop also features a panel on "Semantics and Statistical Machine Translation: Gaps and Challenges" at the end of the program. We invite Eduard Hovy, Percy Liang, Antonio Branco, Quoc V. Le and Chris Quirk as our panel speakers. Semantics-driven machine translation is an emerging and inter-disciplinary direction, which is still in its infancy. The panel discussion will shed light on the future practices and roadmap of semantics-driven machine translation research.

This is the first time that the workshop is held. The success of the workshop relies on a plenty of colleagues involved in this event. We would like to thank the whole Program Committee (30 members) for their invaluable and generous efforts on reviewing the papers this year. We are also very grateful to our invited keynote and panel speakers. Special thanks goes to Prof. Eduard Hovy who suggested the topic of the panel discussion. Additionally, we would like to thank all authors who submitted papers to the workshop. Finally, we acknowledge the general support from our sponsors NiuTrans and the National Science Foundation of China and Jiangsu Province (grants No. 61403269 and BK20140355).

Organizers of the S^2MT workshop
Deyi Xiong, Kevin Duh, Christian Hardmeier and Roberto Navigli

Organizers:

Deyi Xiong (Soochow University)
Kevin Duh (Nara Institute of Science and Technology)
Christian Hardmeier (Uppsala University)
Roberto Navigli (Sapienza University of Rome)

Program Committee:

Francis Bond (Nanyang Technological University)
Johan Bos (University of Groningen)
Ondřej Bojar (Charles University)
Rafael E. Banchs (Institute for Infocomm Research)
Boxing Chen (National Research Council Canada)
JiaJun Chen (Nanjing University)
David Chiang (University of Notre Dame)
Chris Dyer (Carnegie Mellon University)
Spence Green (Stanford University)
Kevin Knight (ISI)
Khalil Sima'an (University of Amsterdam)
Alon Lavie (Carnegie Mellon University)
Quoc V. Le (Google)
Qun Liu (Dublin City University)
Shujie Liu (Microsoft Research Asia)
Yang Liu (Tsinghua University)
Wei Lu (Singapore University of Technology and Design)
Preslav Nakov (Qatar Computing Research Institute)
Martha Palmer (University of Colorado)
Lane Schwartz (University of Illinois)
Xiaodong Shi (Xiamen University)
Linfeng Song (University of Rochester)
Jinsong Su (Xiamen University)
Frances Yung (Nara Institute of Science and Technology)
Jiajun Zhang (Institute of Automation, Chinese Academy of Sciences)
Yue Zhang (Singapore University of Technology and Design)
Tiejun Zhao (Harbin Institute of Technology)
Jinbo Zhu (Northeastern University)
Will Zou (Stanford University)

Additional Reviewers:

Yang Ding (National University of Singapore)

Keynote Speakers:

António Branco (University of Lisbon)
Quoc V. Le (Google)
Percy Liang (Stanford University)

Gerard de Melo (Tsinghua University)

Panelists:

António Branco (University of Lisbon)
Eduard Hovy (Carnegie Mellon University)
Quoc V. Le (Google)
Percy Liang (Stanford University)
Chris Quirk (Microsoft)

Sponsors:

NiuTrans (*http://www.zjyatuo.com/english/*)
National Science Foundation of China (grant No. 61403269)
National Science Foundation of Jiangsu Province (grant No. BK20140355)

Keynote Speech (I)
Semantic Parsing as, via, and for Machine Translation

Percy Liang
Stanford University
pliang@cs.stanford.edu

Abstract

Semantic parsing, the task of mapping natural language sentences to logical forms, has recently played an important role in building natural language interfaces and question answering systems. In this talk, I will present three ways in which semantic parsing relates to machine translation: First, semantic parsing can be viewed ***as*** a translation task with many of the familiar issues, e.g., divergent hierarchical structures. Second, I discuss recent work in which semantic parsing is tackled ***via*** translation (more accurately, paraphrasing) techniques, where original sentences are mapped into canonical sentences encoding the logical form. Finally, I will discuss ways in which semantic parsing could be useful ***for*** translation. Hopefully, this talk will open a deeper dialogue between the semantic parsing and machine translation communities and generate some fresh perspectives on semantics and translation.

Biography

Percy Liang is an Assistant Professor of Computer Science at Stanford University (B.S. from MIT, 2004; Ph.D. from UC Berkeley, 2011). His research interests include (i) modeling natural language semantics, (ii) developing machine learning methods that infer rich latent structures from limited supervision, (iii) and studying the tradeoff between statistical and computational efficiency. He is a 2015 Sloan Research Fellow, 2014 Microsoft Research Faculty Fellow, a 2010 Siebel Scholar, and won the best student paper at the International Conference on Machine Learning in 2008.

Keynote Speech (II)
Learning Multilingual Semantics from Big Data on the Web

Gerard de Melo
IIIS
Tsinghua University
Beijing, China
gdm@demelo.org

Abstract

Over the years, statistical machine translation has gradually shifted from surface form projections to more sophisticated syntactically and to some extent also semantically informed transformations. Still, high-quality semantic analysis of text has to date been a rather elusive goal. Fortunately, unprecedented amounts of Big Data are now readily available via the Web. While genuine semantic interpretation remains challenging, these large quantities of data enable us to develop systems that are more robust and cover a much wider range of concepts and phenomena than those of the past.

Expanding on this idea, I present a series of results on how we can develop systems that learn from Big Data in order to derive better semantic analyses, which in turn have the potential to improve machine translation. These show that it is possible to learn representations that inherit some of the benefits of language-neutral interlingua-like forms, yet preserve language-specific subtleties.

One notable example is UWN (de Melo and Weikum, 2009), a highly multilingual lexical resource allowing us to better cope with lexical gaps and generalize from observed translations. Another one is MENTA, a multilingual knowledge graph describing millions of names and words in over 200 languages in a semantic hierarchy.

The WebChild project (Tandon et al., 2014) mines large amounts of common-sense knowledge from the Web, for instance, that salad is edible and that dogs are capable of barking.

This sort of knowledge extracted from text can additionally be injected into word2vec-style distributed vector representations of words (Chen and de Melo, 2015).

Finally, efforts such as FrameBase (Rouces et al., 2015) harmonize different ways of expressing relationships both in knowledge bases and in text (Čulo and de Melo, 2012).

Biography

Gerard de Melo is a Tenure-Track Assistant Professor at Tsinghua University, Beijing, where he is heading the Web Mining and Language Technology group. He has published over 50 research papers in these areas, being awarded Best Paper awards at CIKM 2010, ICGL 2008, and the NAACL 2015 Workshop on Vector Space Modeling, as well as an ACL 2014 Best Paper Honorable Mention, a Best Student Paper Award nomination at ESWC 2015, and the WWW 2011 Best Demonstration Award, among others. Prior to joining Tsinghua, de Melo had spent two years as a Visiting Scholar at UC Berkeley, working in ICSI's AI/FrameNet group. He received his doctoral degree at the Max Planck Institute for Informatics in Germany. He serves on the Editorial Boards of IEEE Collective Intelligence and of the Language Science Press TMNLP book series. For more information, please refer to his home page at `http://gerard.demelo.org`.

References

Jiaqiang Chen and Gerard de Melo. 2015. Semantic information extraction for improved word embeddings. In Proceedings of the NAACL Workshop on Vector Space Modeling for NLP.

Gerard de Melo and Gerhard Weikum. 2009. Towards a Universal Wordnet by learning from combined evidence. In Proceedings of CIKM 2009.

Jacobo Rouces, Gerard de Melo, and Katja Hose. 2015. Framebase: Representing n-ary relations using semantic frames. In Proceedings of ESWC 2015.

Niket Tandon, Gerard de Melo, Fabian M. Suchanek, and Gerhard Weikum. 2014. Webchild: Harvesting and organizing commonsense knowledge from the web. In Proceedings of ACM WSDM 2014.

Oliver Čulo and Gerard de Melo. 2012. Source-Path- Goal: Investigating the cross-linguistic potential of frame-semantic text analysis. it - Information Technology, 54(3).

Keynote Speech (III)
Sequence to Sequence Learning for Language Understanding

Quoc V. Le
Google
qvl@google.com

Abstract

Most language understanding problems can be formulated as a variable-length input and variable-length output prediction problem. In this talk, I will present a neural network framework to deal with this problem. Our framework makes use of recurrent networks to read in the input sequence of word vectors and predict the output sequence, one token at a time. On our benchmark with WMT'14 our method is as good as with state-of-art phrase based translation methods. I will also present results applying this method to model conversations and generate captions for images.

Biography

Quoc V. Le is one of leading scientists in Deep Learning and Artificial Intelligence, currently working at Google Brain. Quoc obtained his PhD at Stanford, undergraduate degree with First Class Honours and Distinguished Scholar at the Australian National University. He was a researcher at National ICT Australia, Microsoft Research and Max Planck Institute of Biological Cybernetics. Quoc was named one of the innovators under 35 by the MIT Tech Review.

Keynote Speech (IV)
Machine Translation and Deep Language Engineering Approaches

António Branco
University of Lisbon
antonio.branco@di.fc.ul.pt

Abstract

The deeper the processing of utterances the less language-specific differences should remain between the representation of the meaning of a given utterance and the meaning representation of its translation. Further chances of success can thus be explored by machine translation systems that are based on deeper semantic engineering approaches.

Deep language processing has its stepping-stone in linguistically principled methods and generalizations. It has been evolving towards supporting realistic applications, namely by embedding more data based solutions, and by exploring new types of datasets recently developed, such as parallel DeepBanks.

This progress is further supported by recent advances in terms of lexical processing. These advances have been made possible by enhanced techniques for referential and conceptual ambiguity resolution, and supported also by new types of datasets recently developed as linked open data.

In this talk, I will be reporting on the collective work done in the QTLeap project. This is a project that explores novel ways for attaining machine translation of higher quality that we believe are opened by a new generation of increasingly sophisticated semantic datasets and by recent advances in deep language processing.

Biography

António Branco is the Director of the Portuguese node of the CLARIN research infrastructure. He is a professor of language science and technology at the University of Lisbon, where he was the founder and is the head of research of the Natural Language and Speech Group (NLX Group) of the Department of Informatics. He is the (co-)author of over 150 publications in the area of language science and technology and has participated and coordinated several national and international R&D projects. He was the coordinator of the European project METANET4U, integrating the R&D network of excellence META-NET. He is a member of the META-NET Executive Board and he is the first author of the White Paper on the Portuguese Language in the Digital Age.

António Branco is coordinating the QTLeap project (qtleap.eu), an European research project on quality machine translation by deep language engineering approaches.

Table of Contents

Workshop Program

Thursday, July 30, 2015

8:45–9:00	***Opening Remarks***
9:00–10:30	**Session 1**
9:00–10:00	*Keynote Speech (I)* *Semantic Parsing as, via, and for Machine Translation* Percy Liang (Stanford University)
10:00–10:30	*Round trips with meaning stopovers* Alastair Butler
10:30–11:00	***Coffee Break***
11:00–12:30	**Session 2**
11:00–12:00	*Keynote Speech (II)* *Learning Multilingual Semantics from Big Data on the Web* Gerard de Melo (Tsinghua University)
12:00–12:30	*Conceptual Annotations Preserve Structure Across Translations: A French-English Case Study* Elior Sulem, Omri Abend and Ari Rappoport
12:30–13:30	***Lunch***

Thursday, July 30, 2015 (continued)

13:30–15:30	**Session 3**
13:30–14:30	*Keynote Speech (III)* *Sequence to Sequence Learning for Language Understanding* Quoc V. Le (Google)
14:30–15:00	*Integrating Case Frame into Japanese to Chinese Hierarchical Phrase-based Translation Model* Jinan Xu, Jiangming Liu, Yufeng Chen, YUJIE ZHANG, Fang Ming and Shaotong Li
15:00–15:30	*A Discriminative Model for Semantics-to-String Translation* Aleš Tamchyna, Chris Quirk and Michel Galley
15:30–16:00	***Coffee Break***
16:00–17:45	**Session 4**
16:00–17:00	*Keynote Speech (IV)* *Machine Translation and Deep Language Engineering Approaches* António Branco (University of Lisbon)
17:00–17:45	*Panel* *Semantics and Statistical Machine Translation: Gaps and Challenges* Panel Chair: Chris Quirk Panelists: Eduard Hovy, Percy Liang, António Branco, Quoc V. Le
17:45	***Closing***

Round-trips with meaning stopovers

Alastair Butler
Institute for Excellence in Higher Education
Tohoku University
ajb129@hotmail.com

Abstract

This paper describes taking parsed sentences, going to meaning representations (the stopover), and then back to parsed sentences (the round trip). Keeping to the same language tests the combined success of building meaning representations from parsed input and of generating parsed output. Switching languages when manipulating meaning representations would achieve translation. Transfer shortfall is seen with meaning representations built from parsed parallel corpora data, with English-Japanese as an example.

1 Introduction

Recent years have seen progress in the development of open-domain semantic parsers able to convert natural language input to representations that preserve much semantic content (see e.g., Schubert 2015 for an overview). This becomes relevant for translation if there is also a way back to a language string, that is, if there can also be generation from meaning representations. This paper describes a full pipeline: form (Historical) Penn-treebank parsed sentences, a semantic parser is used to create standard predicate logic based meaning representations (see e.g., Dowty, Wall and Peters 1981), which are converted to PENMAN notation (Matthiessen and Bateman 1991) to form the basis for generation, which proceeds as a manipulation of tree structure to produce an output parsed tree which can yield a language string.

The method is illustrated by round tripping on English, so taking English parsed sentences, going to meaning representations, and then back to parsed sentences of English. It is equally possible to change the front or back end of the pipeline, e.g., calculate a meaning representation for an English sentence but use generation rules designed for Japanese. With no modification to the stopover meaning representation this arrives at a result with English words and concepts and yet Japanese parse structure. Obtaining meaning representations from parsed parallel corpora is also illustrated to form the basis for capturing data to inform the gap that remains between the meaning representations needed to generate sentences of one language from another.

The paper is structured as follows. Section 2 discusses related work. Section 3 introduces the semantic parsing to start the pipeline. Section 4 details changes for generation. Section 5 presents results of experiments carried out round tripping on English data. Section 6 discusses the open issue of what remains for translation from one language to another, with an English to Japanese example. Section 7 concludes.

2 Related work

There are many options for reaching what might be called meaning representations. Schubert (2015) is a recent overview of 12 distinct approaches, many with multiple implementations. Of alternatives to section

Proceedings of the 1st Workshop on Semantics-Driven Statistical Machine Translation, pages 1–10,
Beijing, China, July 30, 2015.

3, most closely related is the Boxer system (Bos 2008), which is also part of a pipeline taking parsed input (Boxer uses CCG derivations), and which also implements results of Dynamic Semantics, such as capturing donkey anaphora and handling quantification (see e.g., Eijck and Visser 2012; Boxer uses DRT (Kamp and Reyle 1993), rather than SCT of section 3.2). A notable difference in output is with the linking of predicates: Boxer adopts, in contrast to classical DRT, a neo-Davidsonian approach with information loss for how adjuncts are anchored, posing difficulties for transforming to the PENMAN notation used for generation in section 4. Boxer, the section 3 approach, as well as many others, aim to capture compositional sentence/discourse meaning by building representations with model theoretic embeddings, rather than aiming for a more usage directed "speaker meaning" (see e.g. Bender et al 2015 for a viewpoint against conflating sentence/speaker meaning).

With the approach of this paper, after the meaning representation is reached, much is accomplished with tree transformations. Schubert (2014) is an alternative to building meaning representations from parsed treebank data with only tree transformations, and with a different tree transforming engine (TTT; Purtee and Schubert 2012).

For semantic parsing directly to PENMAN notation, there is JAMR (Flanigan et al 2014), a semantic parser natively producing Abstract Meaning Representations (AMRs; Banarescu et al 2013). JAMR replicates the (by design) limitations of AMR (e.g., sentence outlook, absence of quantification, absence of tense information), and offers AMR advantages of developed predicate senses and semantic roles.

Generation from PENMAN notation is also a well established research area, with notably the Nitrogen system (Langkilde and Knight 1998). Nitrogen relies on a statistical component to filter results generated from a base system with phrase structure like rules. There are other systems with generation from representations of argument structure or quasi-logical forms (e.g., Alshawi 1992, Humphreys et al 2001). The generation of this paper follows a series of transformation rules most similar to those proposed in the generative grammar literature (e.g., Chomsky and Lasnik 1993), which provides the theoretical foundation underlying the treebank annotation of section 3.1. To the knowledge of the author, the system of this paper is the first to bring together components to round trip on languages and evaluate the results based on a metric measuring semantic analysis.

3 Reaching meaning representations

The approach of this paper first requires a way to reach meaning representations from natural language input. Here, use is made of Treebank Semantics (Butler and Yoshimoto 2012, Butler 2015), for the ease with which it fits into the described pipeline, since it takes as input the parsed trees that will be generated as output, and for the quality of meaning representations produced.

Treebank Semantics works by converting parsed constituent tree annotations into expressions of a Dynamic Semantics language (Scope Control Theory or SCT; Butler 2015) which is processed against a sequence based information state (cf. Vermeulen 2000, Dekker 2012) to return predicate logic based representations. Section 3.1 outlines the treebank annotation, while section 3.2 sketches reaching a meaning representation from an example sentence.

3.1 Treebank annotation

The Treebank Semantics system accepts parsed data conforming to the *Annotation manual for the Penn Historical Corpora and the PCEEC* (Santorini 2010). This widely and diversely applied scheme forms the basis of annotations for over 600,000 analysed sentences of English (Taylor et al 2003, Kroch, Santorini and Delfs 2004,

Kroch, Santorini and Delfs 2004), French (Martineau et al 2010), Icelandic (Wallenberg et al 2011), Portuguese (Galves and Britto 2002), Ancient Greek (Beck 2013), Japanese (Butler et al 2012), and Chinese (Zhou 2015) among other languages, and has parsing systems to produce annotated trees from raw language input (e.g., Kulick, Kroch and Santorini 2014, Fang, Butler and Yoshimoto 2014).

With the annotation scheme constituent structure is represented with labelled bracketing and augmented with grammatical functions and notation for recovering discontinuous constituents. A parse in tree form for the sentence *Pizza that I made was delicious* looks like:

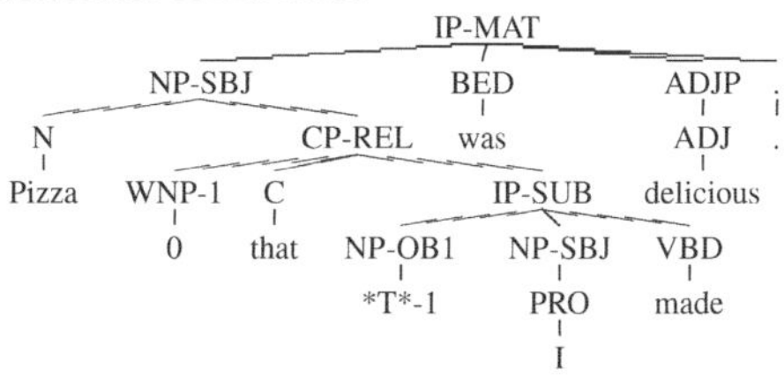

Every word has a word level part-of-speech label. Phrasal nodes (NP, PP, ADJP, etc.) immediately dominate the phrase head (N, P, ADJ, etc.), so that the phrase head has as sisters both modifiers and complements. Modifiers and complements are distinguished by extended phrase labels marking function (e.g., CP-REL above encodes *that I made* is a relative clause, and so a modifier of the head noun *Pizza*). All noun phrases immediately dominated by IP are marked for function (NP-SBJ=subject, NP-OB1=direct object, NP-TMP=temporal NP, etc.). All clauses have extended labels to mark function (IP-MAT=matrix clause, CP-ADV=adverbial clause, etc.). There can be additional annotation containing scope information to ensure an unambiguous parse with respect to a default scope hierarchy.

3.2 Obtaining meaning representations

To obtain meaning representations, the first step is to convert a labelled bracketed tree into an expression to input to the SCT evaluation system. An SCT expression is built exploiting the input phrase structure by locating any complement for the phrase head to scope over, and adding modifiers as elements that scope above the head. During construction information about binding names is gathered and integrated with `fn fh =>` and `fn lc =>` acting as lambda abstractions. As a demonstration, the tree of section 3.1 converts as follows:

```
val ex1 =
( fn fh =>
  ( fn lc =>
    ( some lc fh "entity"
      ( relc lc "q1"
        ( pro fh "I" "arg0"
          ( arg "q1" "arg1"
            ( past "event"
              ( verb lc "event"
                 ["arg0", "arg1"] "made"))))
        ( nn lc "Pizza"))
      "arg0"
      ( some lc fh "attrib" ( adj lc "delicious")
        "attribute"
        ( past "event"
          ( verb lc "event" ["arg0"] "was")))))
  ["attribute", "arg1", "arg0"])
["event", "entity", "attrib"]
```

This conversion to `ex1` notably transforms into operations the part of speech tags given by the nodes immediately dominating the terminals of the input constituent tree (`some` (indefinite) `nn` (noun), `verb`, `arg` (trace), etc.), as well as triggering operations for certain construction types (e.g., `relc` occurs because there is a relative clause). Conversion also adds (i) information about local binding names (e.g., `"arg0"` (logical subject role), `"arg1"` (logical object role), `"attribute"`), and (ii) information about sources for fresh bindings (e.g., `"event"`, `"entity"` and `"attrib"`) for the introduction of variables of different sorts. The created operations further reduce to primitives of the SCT language as demonstrated with:

```
Hide ("event",
 Close ("∃", ("entity","entity"),["event", "entity", "attrib"],
   ...
    Lam ("q1", "arg1",
     If (fn,
      Use ("event",
       If (fn,
        Rel ([], [], "made", [At (T ("arg0", 0), "arg0"),
         At (T ("arg1", 0), "arg1"),
         At (T ("event", 0), "event")]),
        ...
```

The SCT language primitives access and possibly alter the content of a sequence based information state that serves to retain binding information by assigning (possibly empty) sequences of values to binding names, notably: `Use` (triggers quantification introduction), `Hide` (occludes `Use`), `At` (constructs argument,role pairs), `Close` (quantificational closure), `Rel` (constructs relations), `If` (conditional to select what is evaluated), and `Lam` (shifts bindings between binding names). Evaluation of the resulting SCT expression conspires to bring about the enforcement of fixed roles on the binding names from the conversion of the parsed constituent tree annotation (`"arg0"`, `"arg1"`, `"attrib"`, etc.).

With evaluation of `ex1`, the following meaning representation is returned:

$\exists z_4 x_1 A_5 e_2 e_3$ (
  past (e_2) $\wedge$
    past (e_3) $\wedge$
      delicious (A_5) $\wedge$
        made (e_2, z_4, x_1) $\wedge$ pizza (x_1) $\wedge$
          $z_4 = \mathrm{I} \wedge$ was (e_3, x_1, A_5))

This assumes a Davidsonian theory (Davidson 1967) in which verbs are encoded with minimally an implicit event argument which is existentially quantified over and may be further modified. Such a meaning representation encodes truth-conditional content in a standard way, but also contains clues to assist generation. Most notably variables have sort information, thus: $e_1, e_2, \ldots$ are events, $x_1, x_2, \ldots$ are objects, $A_1, A_2, \ldots$ are attributes, etc. Also, the main predicate is the most deeply embedded right-side predicate.

4 Generation

The idea behind the approach to generation is, from a meaning representation presented as a tree, to follow a series of meaning preserving transformations to arrive back at a parsed syntactic representation, that is, to a representation of the kind fed to the Treebank Semantics system at the start of the pipeline. There are two major steps. First, there is preparation, discussed in section 4.1, and subsequently there is generation, demonstrated in section 4.2 as building and transforming tree structure.

4.1 Preparing for generation

Preparation for generation involves obtaining an alternative tree-based representation of the output produced by Treebank Semantics. Rendering the meaning representation of section 3.2 as a tree with argument role information made explicit gives:

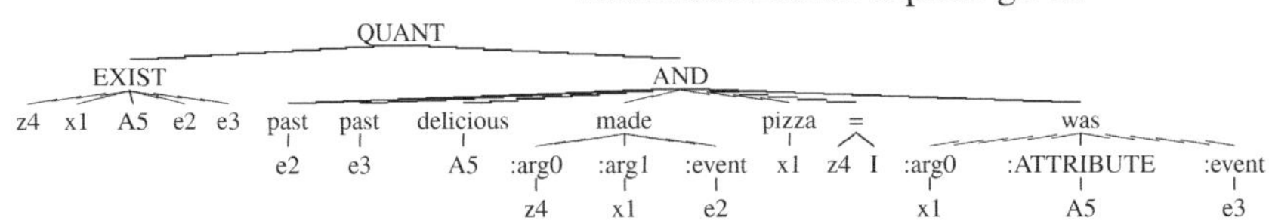

Content is further re-packaged to a tree format optimised for generation. Firstly, the binding of wide-scope existentials is made implicit with the removal of the top quantification level. Next, an argument of each predicate is promoted to become the parent of the predicate, notably: the left-hand argument of an equality relation, or an `event` argument if present, or the sole argument of a one-place predicate.

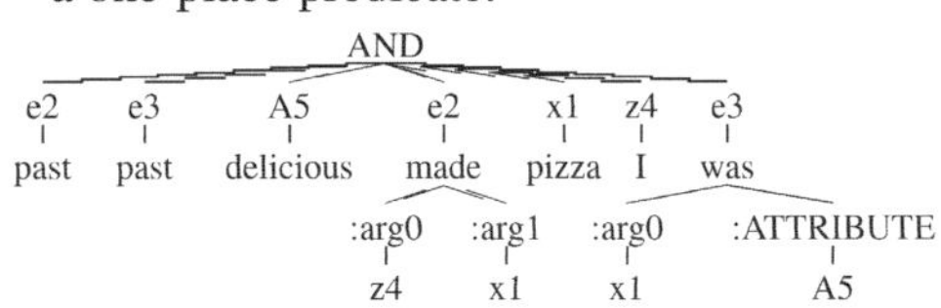

Next, a daughter D of the top level AND is moved inside a sister S when the argument name at the root of D is contained as an argument within S. Movement is to only one location (the left-most).

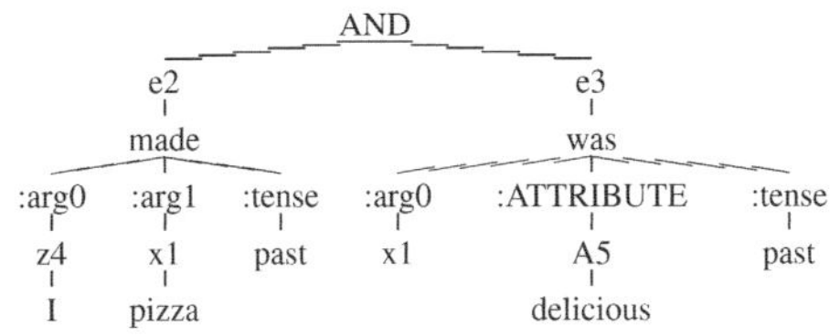

An internal argument is promoted to become the root of a daughter of AND if this enables further inclusion into a sister. Promotion relies on folding tree material around inverse roles from the PENMAN notation (Matthiessen and Bateman 1991), e.g., having `arg1-of` as an inverse of `arg1` (logical object) enables transformation to the following single rooted structure, and more generally compacts long distance dependencies such as are established as WH-dependencies in English:

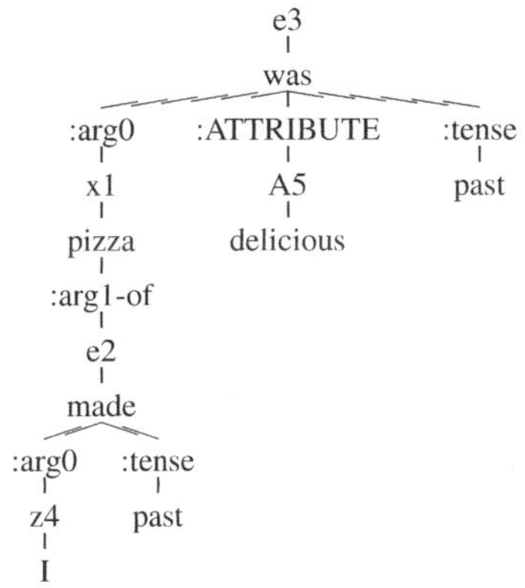

4.2 Back to a parsed representation

Representations resulting from the changes of the previous section are now used as the basis for generation. This proceeds as a series of tree transformations, implemented as a tsurgeon script (Levy and Andrew 2006) with hundreds of transformation rules.

A tsurgeon script contains pattern/action rules, where the pattern describes tree structure and the action transforms the tree, e.g., moving, adjoining, copying or deleting auxiliary trees or relabelling nodes. Transformations are repeatedly made until the pattern that triggers change is no longer matched. Thus, clause structure is built by identifying a main predicate as being headed by an event variable (so: match *e* followed by a number), and adjoining the projection of a VBP part-of-speech tag, a VP layer and an IP layer.

```
/^e[0-9]+$/=x !> VBP

adjoinF (IP (VP (VBP @))) x
```

Action `adjoinF` adjoins the specified auxiliary tree into the specified target node, preserving the target node as the foot of the adjoined tree. VBP (present tense verb) may subsequently change, e.g., `tense past` triggers change to VBD (past tense verb), while *was* when generating English brings about further change to BED (past tense copula).

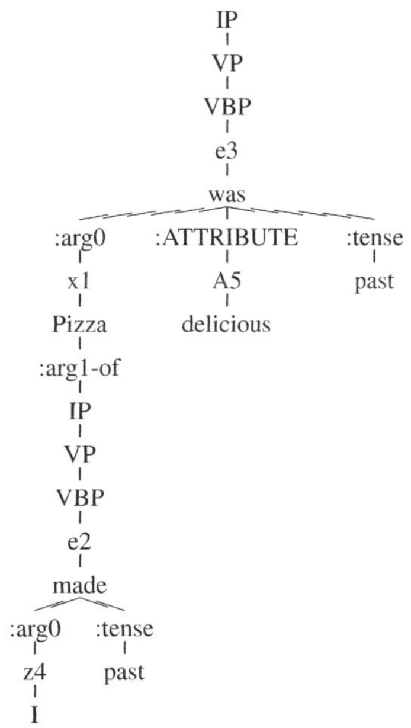

Subsequent changes involve moving all structure under a main predicate into the clause, starting with the creation of NP-SBJ from an `arg0` argument at the IP-level.

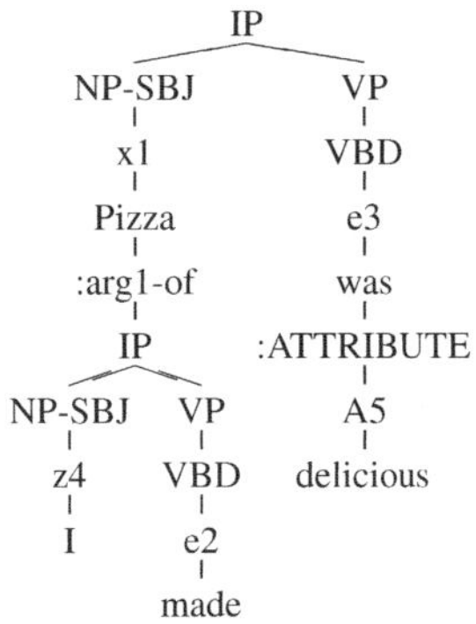

The inverse role `arg1-of` is the foundation for relative clause structure with an NP-OB1 (object) trace, while if pizza had been headed by an event variable, the structure would bring about a clausal embedding.

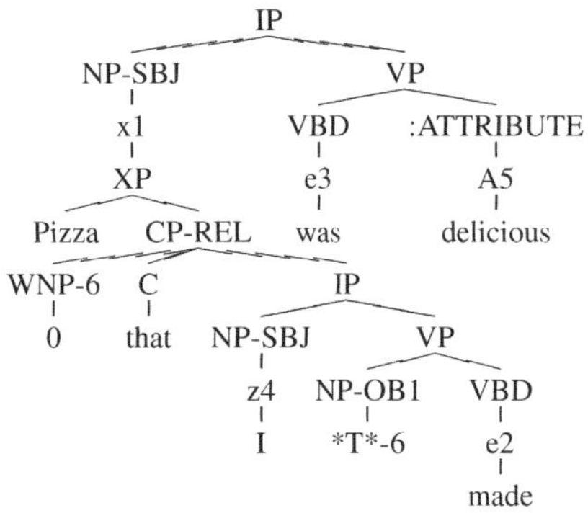

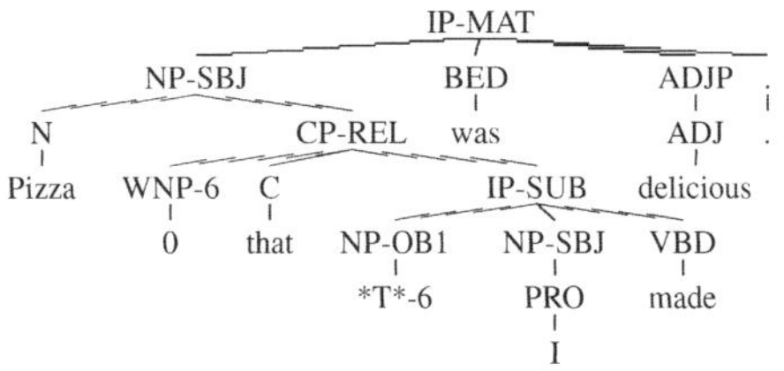

If an `arg0` argument happened to be missing, either a passive transformation may result or there may be inclusion of a subject expletive *it* or *there* for English. Adjunct materials can find placement based on argument role information or subtree size, e.g., vocatives (NP-VOC) are always clause initial, a temporal NP (NP-TMP) will typically be clause initial, while, for English, clause final positioning will be favoured for a heavy PP or NP (whose children reach large depths). Having arguments with the same referent can trigger the introduction of infinitival or participial clause structure to create control configurations or various types of ellipsis, such as VP ellipsis.

5 Experiments

In this section, the smatch metric for measuring semantic annotation agreement rates and semantic parsing accuracy (Cai and Knight 2013) is used to evaluate the success of round tripping on English. This is a metric to measure whole-sentence semantic analysis by calculating the degree of overlap between meaning representations.

The representation seen at the end of section 4.1 is essentially compatible for calculating a smatch score. This gives a meaning representation for the input sentence. A meaning representation for the output sentence is achieved by feeding the resulting output of the round trip back into the Treebank Semantics system.

Table 1 details results for 1452 annotated sentences (14,118 tokens) from four different registers that were manually selected to illustrate different levels of sentence complexity. All sentences are from the Treebank Semantics Corpus[1] with sentences parsed to gold standard following the annotation scheme detailed in section 3.1, and so already unambiguous for feeding to

register	sentences	tokens	precision	recall	F-score
textbook	687	5194	0.98	0.98	0.98
newswire	121	2381	0.97	0.96	0.97
(simple) fiction	547	5241	0.96	0.96	0.96
non-fiction	97	1302	0.93	0.93	0.93

Table 1: smatch scores comparing meaning representations from original and generated sentences

[1] `https://github.com/ajb129/tscorpus`

the semantic component for the creation of a gold standard meaning representation.

The results show that in round tripping with English, so building a meaning representation A and generating back to an English sentence and then building a meaning representation B from the generated sentence, and then comparing A with B, it is possible to retain the bulk of semantic content with high precision and recall.

The results also reflect that performance starts to decline on more challenging data. In particular there is a notable reduction in F-score with the non-fiction data (from a technical manual describing the IBM 1401 Programming System). Weaknesses revealed typically involve complex interactions, such as happen with coordination, or stem from constructions that are difficult to provide a generalisable semantic analysis, such as comparatives. On the generation side, improvements are possible with more construction and lexical specific pattern/action rules, reordering existing rules, or arranging for existing rules to be retriggered.

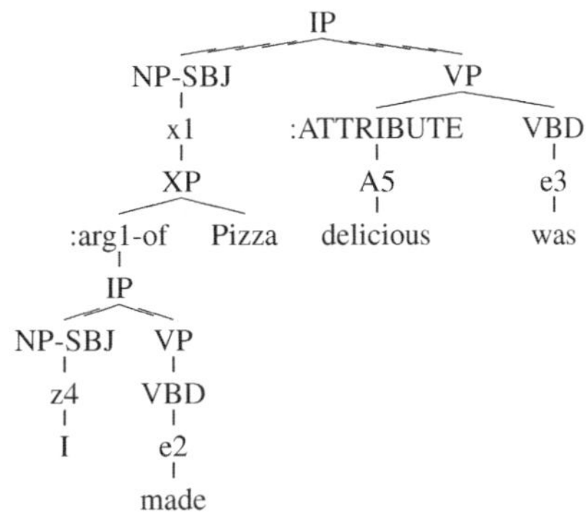

Projection of relative clause structure is again triggered, only for Japanese there is projection of an IP-REL layer to the left side of the head noun.

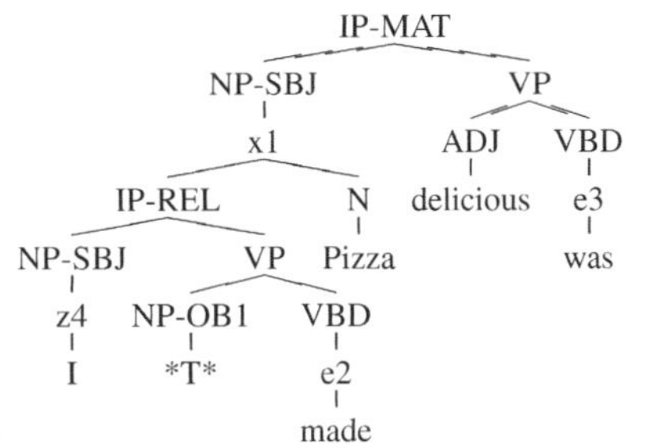

6 Towards translation

In this section, generation rules for Japanese are demonstrated. Consider starting with the same meaning representation input as section 4.2, and first projecting VP, IP structure. Thereafter rules diverge, differing mostly in terms of constituent placement.

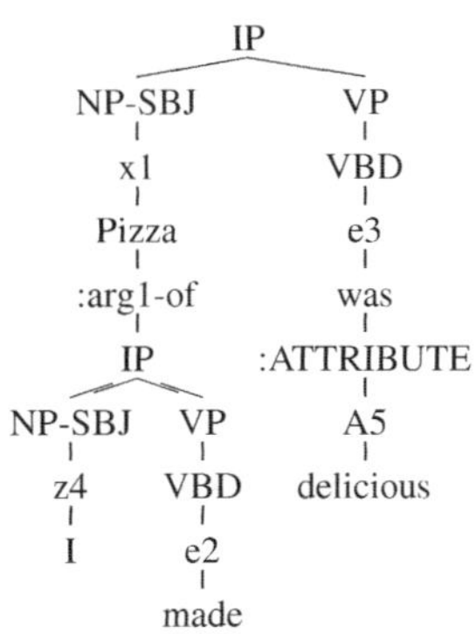

Generation is completed with the addition of case particles.

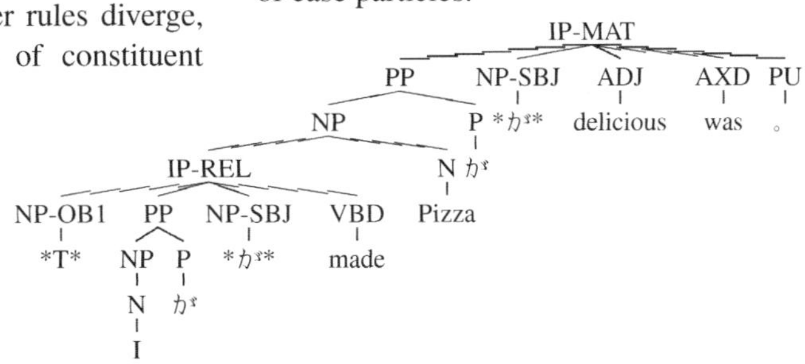

This has demonstrated generation to Japanese parse structure from a meaning representation with English words and concepts. In the case of this illustrative example there is a close match with the corresponding Japanese version 僕が作ったピザがおいしかったです, seen annotated below. However, for the general translation task, substantial transformation and lexical substitution of the meaning representation used for generation will be required.

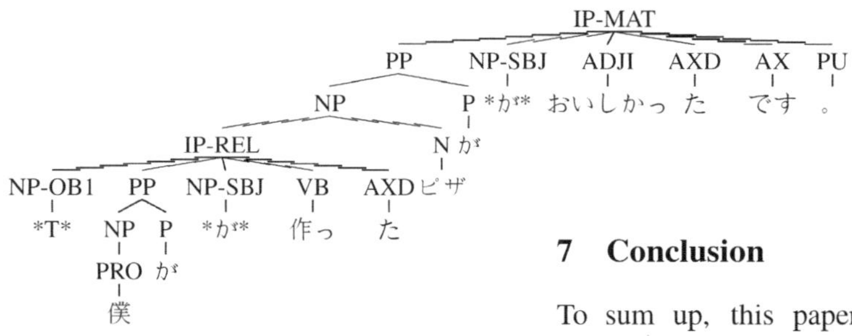

By feeding the Japanese version of the example sentence into to the Treebank Semantics system a meaning representation is built:

$\exists x_4 x_1 e_2 e_3$ (
past(e_3) ∧
past(e_2) ∧
x_4 = 僕 ∧
作っ_た(e_2, x_4, x_1) ∧
ピザ(x_1) ∧
おいしかっ_た_です(e_3, x_1))

Such a representation can be modified, as in section 4.1, to form the basis for generation, exactly as with the English example.

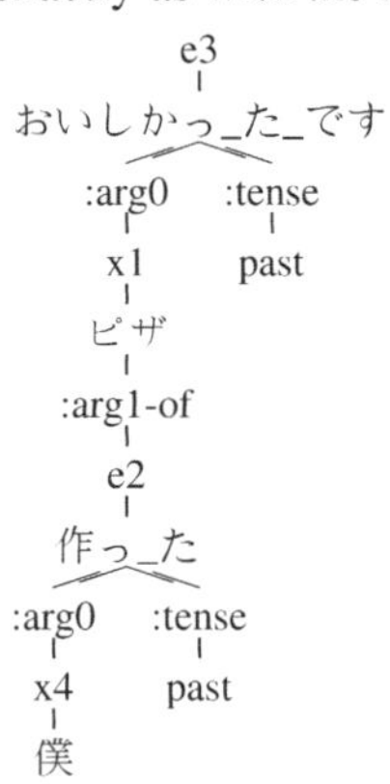

Having the above meaning representation and the meaning representation for the corresponding English sentence in section 4.1, together with meaning representations for other sentences of parallel corpora, is a basis for extracting rules for a full translation system.

7 Conclusion

To sum up, this paper has described a complete pipeline for taking parsed sentences, going to meaning representations (initially to standard Davidsonian predicate logic based meaning representations, then to PENMAN notation), and then back to parsed sentences (the round trip). Keeping to the same language tests the combined success of building meaning representations from parsed input and of generating parsed output. Using the smatch metric reveals that the bulk of semantic content is retained with high precision and recall on a range of data.

Results show that, while there is no explicit flagging in a conventional Davidsonian predicate logic meaning representation, as seen in section 3.2, of what is a verb, noun, adjective, relative clause, passive, control relation, etc., much information is found to facilitate generation when there is sort and argument role information and when there is subsequent re-packaging of content, as in section 4.1, guided by the aim to form single rooted structures.

The future direction for this research is to show relevance for translation in being able to switch languages at the point of manipulating meaning representations. Current transfer shortfall is seen with meaning representations built from parsed parallel corpora data.

Acknowledgements

This paper benefitted considerably from the comments of three anonymous reviewers, as well as discussions with Pascual Martínez-Gómez, Masaaki Nagata, Kei Yoshimoto and Zhen Zhou, all of which is very gratefully acknowledged. This research is supported by the Japan Society for the Promotion of Science (JSPS), Research Project Number: 15K02469.

References

Alshawi, Hiyan. 1992. *The Core Language Engine*. Cambridge, Mass.: MIT Press.

Banarescu, L., C. Bonial, S. Cai, M. Georgescu, K. Griffitt, U. Hermjakob, K. Knight, P. Koehn, M. Palmer, and N. Schneider. 2013. Abstract Meaning Representation for Sembanking. In *Proceedings of the 7th Linguistic Annotation Workshop and Interoperability with Discourse*, pages 178–186.

Beck, Jana E. 2013. Annotation manual for the Penn parsed corpora of Historical Greek. Tech. rep., Department of Computer and Information Science, University of Pennsylvania, Philadelphia.

Bender, Emily M., Dan Flickinger, Stephan Oepen, Woodley Packard, and Ann Copestake. 2015. Layers of interpretation: On grammar and compositionality. In *Proceedings of the 11th International Conference on Computational Semantics*, pages 239–249. London, UK: Association for Computational Linguistics.

Bos, Johan. 2008. Wide-coverage semantic analysis with Boxer. In J. Bos and R. Delmonte, eds., *Semantics in Text Processing. STEP 2008 Conference Proceedings*, Research in Computational Semantics, pages 277–286. College Publications.

Butler, Alastair. 2015. *Linguistic Expressions and Semantic Processing: A Practical Approach*. Heidelberg: Springer-Verlag.

Butler, Alastair, Zhu Hong, Tomoko Hotta, Ruriko Otomo, Kei Yoshimoto, and Zhen Zhou. 2012. Keyaki treebank: phrase structure with functional information for Japanese. In *Proceedings of Text Annotation Workshop*.

Butler, Alastair and Kei Yoshimoto. 2012. Banking meaning representations from treebanks. *Linguistic Issues in Language Technology - LiLT* 7(1):1–22.

Cai, Shu and Kevin Knight. 2013. Smatch: an evaluation metric for semantic feature structures. In *Proc. of the ACL 2013*.

Chomsky, Noam and Howard Lasnik. 1993. The theory of Principles and Parameters. In J. Jacobs, ed., *Syntax: An International Handbook of Contemporary Research*. Berlin: Walter de Gruyter.

Davidson, Donald. 1967. The logical form of action sentences. In N. Rescher, ed., *The Logic of Decision and Action*. Pittsburgh: University of Pittsburgh Press. Reprinted in: D. Davidson, 1980. *Essays on Actions and Events*. Claredon Press, Oxford, pages 105–122.

Dekker, Paul. 2012. *Dynamic Semantics*, vol. 91 of *Studies in Linguistics and Philosophy*. Dordrecht: Springer Verlag.

Dowty, David, Robert Wall, and Stanley Peters. 1981. *Introduction to Montague Semantics*. Dordrecht: Kluwer.

Eijck, Jan van and Albert Visser. 2012. Dynamic Semantics. In E. N. Zalta, ed., *The Stanford Encyclopedia of Philosophy*. Winter 2012 edn.

Fang, Tsaiwei, Alastair Butler, and Kei Yoshimoto. 2014. Parsing Japanese with a PCFG treebank grammar. In *Proceedings of the Twentieth Annual Meeting of the Association of Natural Language Processing*, pages 432–435. Sapporo, Japan.

Flanigan, Jeffrey, Sam Thomson, Jaime Carbonell, Chris Dyer, and Noah A. Smith. 2014. A discriminative graph-based parser for the abstract meaning representation. In *Proc. of the ACL 2014*.

Galves, Charlotte and Helena Britto. 2002. *The Tycho Brahe Corpus of Historical Portuguese*. Department of Linguistics, University of Campinas. Online publication, first edition.

Humphreys, Kevin, Mike Calcagno, and David Weise. 2001. Reusing a statistical language model for generation. In *Proceedings of the 8th European workshop on Natural Language Generation - Volume 8*, pages 1–6. Stroudsburg, PA: Association for Computational Linguistics.

Kamp, Hans and Uwe Reyle. 1993. *From Discourse to Logic: Introduction to Modeltheoretic Semantics of Natural Language, Formal Logic and Discourse Representation Theory*. Dordrecht: Kluwer.

Kroch, Anthony, Beatrice Santorini, and Lauren Delfs. 2004. *The Penn-Helsinki Parsed Corpus of Early Modern English (PPCEME)*. Department of Linguistics, University of Pennsylvania. CD-ROM, first edition.

Kulick, Seth, Anthony Kroch, and Beatrice Santorini. 2014. The Penn parsed corpus of Modern British English: First parsing results and analysis. In *Proceedings of the 52nd Annual Meeting of the Association for Computational Linguistics (Short Papers)*, pages 662–667. Baltimore, Maryland, USA: Association for Computational Linguistics.

Langkilde, Irene and Kevin Knight. 1998. Generation that exploits corpus-based statistical knowledge. In *Proceedings of the ACL/COLING-98*. Montreal, Quebéc.

Levy, Roger and Galen Andrew. 2006. Tregex and tsurgeon: tools for querying and manipulating tree data structure. In *5th International conference on Language Resources and Evaluation*.

Martineau, France, Paul Hirschbühler, Anthony Kroch, and Yves Charles Morin. 2010. *Corpus MCVF (parsed corpus), Modéliser le changement : les voies du français*. Département de français, University of Ottawa. CD-ROM, first edition.

Matthiessen, Christian and John A Bateman. 1991. *Text generation and systemic-functional linguistics: experiences from English and Japanese*. Pinter Publishers.

Purtee, A. and Lenhart K. Schubert. 2012. TTT: A tree transduction language for syntactic and semantic processing. In *EACL 2012 Workshop on Applications of Tree Automata Techniques in Natural Language Processing (ATANLP 2012)*. Avignon, France.

Santorini, Beatrice. 2010. Annotation manual for the Penn Historical Corpora and the PCEEC (Release 2). Tech. rep., Department of Computer and Information Science, University of Pennsylvania, Philadelphia.

Schubert, Lenhart K. 2014. From treebank parses to episodic logic and commonsense inference. In *Proc. of the ACL 2014 Workshop on Semantic Parsing*, pages 55–60. Baltimore, MD.

Schubert, Lenhart K. 2015. Semantic representation. In *29th AAAI Conference (AAAI15)*, pages 55–60. Austin, TX.

Taylor, Ann, Anthony Warner, Susan Pintzuk, and Frank Beths. 2003. *The York-Toronto-Helsinki Parsed Corpus of Old English Prose (YCOE)*. Department of Linguistics, University of York. Oxford Text Archive, first edition.

Vermeulen, C. F. M. 2000. Variables as stacks: A case study in dynamic model theory. *Journal of Logic, Language and Information* 9:143–167.

Wallenberg, Joel, Anton Karl Ingason, Einar Freyr Sigurðsson, and Eiríkur Rögnvaldsson. 2011. *Icelandic Parsed Historical Corpus (IcePaHC)*. Department of Linguistics, University of Iceland. Online publication, version 0.9.

Zhou, Zhen. 2015. *Parsing Chinese for Semantic Processing: Focusing on Serial Verb Constructions and Resultative Constructions*. Ph.D. thesis, Tohoku University, Sendai, Japan.

Conceptual Annotations Preserve Structure Across Translations: A French-English Case Study

Elior Sulem
Institute of Computer Science
Hebrew University of Jerusalem
eliors@cs.huji.ac.il

Omri Abend
School of Informatics
University of Edinburgh
oabend@inf.ed.ac.uk

Ari Rappoport
Institute of Computer Science
Hebrew University of Jerusalem
arir@cs.huji.ac.il

Abstract

Divergence of syntactic structures between languages constitutes a major challenge in using linguistic structure in Machine Translation (MT) systems. Here, we examine the potential of *semantic* structures. While semantic annotation is appealing as a source of cross-linguistically stable structures, little has been accomplished in demonstrating this stability through a detailed corpus study. In this paper, we experiment with the UCCA conceptual-cognitive annotation scheme in an English-French case study. First, we show that UCCA can be used to annotate French, through a systematic type-level analysis of the major French grammatical phenomena. Second, we annotate a parallel English-French corpus with UCCA, and quantify the similarity of the structures on both sides. Results show a high degree of stability across translations, supporting the usage of semantic annotations over syntactic ones in structure-aware MT systems.

1 Introduction

Structural information, be it syntactic or semantic, has the potential to address long-standing problems in Statistical Machine Translation (SMT), such as phrase-level (rather than word-level) reordering and discontiguous phrases. Structure-aware models[1] (Chiang, 2005; Liu et al., 2006; Mi et al., 2008) aim to address these and other problems by taking into account the hierarchical structure of language. However, while structure-aware models are effective at improving reordering at the phrase level, they are limited in their ability to map between arbitrarily divergent structures. Cross-linguistic divergences therefore pose a difficult problem for the integration of structural knowledge into statistical models (Dorr, 1994; Ding and Palmer, 2004; Zhang et al., 2008).

Consequently, an annotation scheme that assigns similar structures to translations has direct applicative value for structure-aware MT systems. Such structures can be used either as features in phrase-based systems, yielding more robust decoding, or as a structural scheme which directs the translation, replacing the PCFG trees often used today. Using more stable schemes is likely to result in simpler MT systems, avoiding structure modifications like pseudo-nodes (Marcu et al., 2006) or tree sequences (Zhang et al., 2008) used in syntax-based systems to handle cross-linguistic divergences.

Semantic annotation is an appealing avenue for constructing cross-linguistically stable structures, since a major goal of translation is to preserve the meaning of a sentence. Cross-linguistically stable schemes have further benefits for applications such as knowledge projection across languages (Kozhevnikov and Titov, 2013), the induction of cross-lingual semantic relations (Lewis and Steedman, 2013), or in translation studies (Lembersky et al., 2013) (see Section 7.3). A recent example of a semantic scheme aiming to be cross-linguistically stable is AMR (Abstract Meaning Representation) (Banarescu et al., 2013) which uses elaborate hierarchical structures in order to abstractly represent semantic information and presents promising preliminary results for SMT improvement (Jones et al., 2012). Nevertheless, the stability of semantic annotation across

[1]We use the term "structure-aware" rather than "syntax-based" so to include any type of hierarchical structure.

Proceedings of the 1st Workshop on Semantics-Driven Statistical Machine Translation, pages 11–22,
Beijing, China, July 30, 2015. ©2015 Association for Computational Linguistics

translations is seldom addressed and has yet to be adequately supported (see Section 2), a gap we address in this paper using a detailed analysis of a semantically annotated parallel corpus.

Universal Cognitive Conceptual Annotation (UCCA) is a coarse-grained semantic annotation scheme which builds on typological and cognitive linguistic theory (Abend and Rappoport, 2013a; Abend and Rappoport, 2013b). The scheme aims to be applicable cross-linguistically, to abstract away from specific syntactic forms and to directly represent semantic distinctions. These properties make UCCA an appealing source of structural annotation which is cross-linguistically stable. We give an overview of UCCA in Section 3.

This paper focuses on the case study of English-French, a well studied language pair in MT. We demonstrate through this language pair both UCCA's *portability*, namely its ability to be applied to different languages, and its *stability*, namely its ability to preserve structure across translations. We conduct both type-level and token-level experiments to support our claim.

To verify UCCA's portability to French, we first conduct a type-level analysis by systematically examining UCCA's applicability over all major grammatical phenomena in French. We find that UCCA is fully applicable to French as exemplified in the case of French-specific phenomena like pronominal verbs (Section 4.1). Further in the type-level, we apply UCCA to a published inventory of structural divergences, and find that UCCA abstracts away from almost all of them (Section 4.2).

For a token-level analysis, we manually UCCA-annotated a parallel French-English corpus of over 25K tokens, which we make publically available, and compare the similarity between the UCCA structures in the two languages to the corresponding similarity between syntactic annotations. We find that UCCA is considerably less divergent than syntactic annotation (Section 6). We expect the relative stability of UCCA compared to syntactic schemes to be even greater in language pairs that are more syntactically different than the relatively similar English-French.

Finally, we analyze the semantic correspondence between the annotations on both sides of the parallel corpus (Section 7). We find remarkably high semantic correspondence between the two languages. For instance, over 92% of the Scenes (a similar notion to a "frame"; see Section 3) in both languages have a correspondent in the other. We analyze the non-corresponding units in the two languages according to various parameters, and show that many of them are due to ambiguity or semantic changes. These results offer a better understanding of UCCA's stability and suggest paths for further improvements.

2 Related Work

We begin by discussing previous work that studied the portability and stability of semantic schemes. We then briefly survey the means in which semantic information is integrated into MT systems.

Portability of semantic annotation. Several works addressed the portability of semantic annotation schemes, namely whether the same scheme, often originally developed for English, can be applied to other languages.

Burchardt et al. (2009) addressed the application of the English FrameNet (Baker et al., 1998) to German. They found that about a third of the verb senses identified in the German corpus were not covered by FrameNet. Their analysis further revealed that the English category set is not always sufficient, resulting in the introduction of a new category for German. Van der Plas et al. (2010) addressed the application of English PropBank (Palmer et al., 2005) to French, and found that while the scheme can be applied to French, the annotation requires proficiency in both languages. Samardzic et al. (2010a; 2010b) also studied the portability of the English PropBank to French, and found that the overwhelming majority of the French verbal predicates in the corpus correspond to a verb sense in the PropBank lexicon. The portability of PropBank was also examined in the case of English-Chinese through the construction of annotated parallel corpora used in the OntoNotes project (Weischedel et al., 2012).

Portability has also been studied in the context of more elaborate hierarchical structures (Dorr et al., 2010; Banarescu et al., 2013), often with the intention of producing an *inter-language* – a representation independent of any specific language, which exhaustively accounts for the meaning of the sentence. Dorr et al. (2010) studied portability through the construction of a set of annotated parallel corpora in six languages, as part of the IAMTC project. Portability has also been investigated through the construction of annotated parallel treebanks such as the Prague Czech-English

Dependency Treebank[2], enabling a subsequent valency stability study (Urešová et al., 2015).

Stability of semantic annotation. Another line of work focused on the stability of specific schemes, i.e., their ability to preserve structure across translations. Fung et al. (2006; 2007) studied the stability of semantic role annotation between arguments in English and Chinese. They found that 83% of the alignable verbal arguments in English have a role-compatible argument in Chinese, but did not address arguments that have no correspondent in the other language. This motivated the use of semantic roles in MT, but also highlighted the existence of divergences between the structures in the two languages.

Semantic role schemes used in MT are generally restricted to verbal predicates, excluding several highly frequent constructions, such as copula clauses and nominalizations, which can result in a loss of stability. Furthermore, the fine-grained information such schemes provide as to the role of the arguments can be difficult to port across languages. For further discussion, see (Abend and Rappoport, 2013b) and (Birch et al., 2013).

Abstract Meaning Representation (AMR) (Banarescu et al., 2013) is a hierarchical semantic representation scheme whose aim is to provide simple, readable semantic annotation that can be applied cross-linguistically and assist MT systems. While UCCA is encoded over the text, AMR provides a structure for each sentence that is not trivially alignable with the text (Flanigan et al., 2014). Xue et al. (2014) studied the scheme's portability and stability when applied to English-Chinese and English-Czech parallel corpora. They annotated 100 Chinese and Czech sentences translated from English, and examined the similarities and differences of the AMRs across translations. In the English-Czech comparison, 53% of the sentences are reported to be structurally different in a non-local way. They conclude that at this point AMR is not stable enough to be used as an interlanguage, but should be used only either on the target or on the source side.

Focusing on closer languages, namely English-French, we employ both type-level and token-level approaches for UCCA, including a comparison to syntax and a qualitative analysis of divergences, which are likely to generalize to some extent to other semantic annotations. We report a preliminary study of the stability of AMR in our corpus.

Integrating semantics into MT systems. Widely used in early MT (Uchida, 1987; Nirenburg, 1989), the integration of semantics into SMT systems is receiving much renewed interest in recent years. The first line of research is the integration of semantic features (often semantic roles) in SMT systems. In the phrase-based SMT models, they were mainly utilized for influencing reordering (Wu and Fung, 2009; Xiong et al., 2012; Feng et al., 2012). In syntax-based SMT models, semantic roles were involved in assisting reordering models (Li et al., 2013) and in translation rules (Zhai et al., 2012; Liu and Gildea, 2010; Bazrafshan and Gildea, 2013).

The second line of research concerns the use of an inter-language as an intermediary representation in SMT. Edelman and Solan (2009), relying on the cognitive model Revised Hierarchical Model (RHM), tried to represent the network of constructions that mediates between concepts and the channels of linguistic input and output. Jones et al. (2012) conducted preliminary experiments on a geographical querying domain using AMR.

3 UCCA Annotation

UCCA is a a semantic annotation scheme, strongly influenced by typological, notably Basic Linguistic Theory (Dixon, 2010a; Dixon, 2010b; Dixon, 2012), and cognitive linguistic theories (Langacker, 2008). The scheme aims to provide a coarse-grained, cross-linguistically applicable representation by directly reflecting the major semantic phenomena represented in the text and abstracting away from specific syntactic forms. We briefly introduce the UCCA formalism and main categories. For a more elaborate presentation, as well as evidence for the accessibility of UCCA to annotators with no linguistic background, see (Abend and Rappoport, 2013a; Abend and Rappoport, 2013b).

UCCA structures are directed acyclic graphs, where the words in the text correspond to (a subset of) their leaves. The nodes of the graphs, called *units*, are either terminals or several elements jointly viewed as a single entity according to some semantic or cognitive consideration. The edges bear one or more categories, indicating the role of the sub-unit in the relation that the parent represents.

UCCA is built as a multi-layered scheme, where each layer represents a different set of distinc-

[2]https://ufal.mff.cuni.cz/pcedt2.0/

tions. In this work we use the foundational layer of UCCA, which mostly addresses predicate-argument structures and linkage relations between them.

UCCA views the text as a collection of *Scenes* and relations between them. A Scene, the most basic notion of this layer, describes a movement, an action or a state which is persistent in time. Every Scene contains one main relation, or anchor (similar to frame-evoking element in FrametNet), and is labeled as a *State* (S) or a *Process* (P).

A Scene may contain one or more *Participants* (A), which are interpreted in a broad sense, and include locations, destinations and complement clauses. Secondary relations in the Scene, such as manner or temporal descriptions, are labeled as *Adverbials* (D). For example, the sentence "He slowly ran into the park" is annotated as follows: "[He]$_A$ [slowly]$_D$ [ran]$_P$ [into the park]$_A$".

The definitions of the UCCA categories are not dependent on POS distinctions. For instance, a Scene's main relation can be an adjective ("[He]$_A$ ['s thin]$_S$") or a noun ("[John 's]$_A$ [decision]$_P$").

4 Type-Level Analysis

In this section we focus on type-level analysis and show both the portability of UCCA, examining the annotation of the French grammatical phenomena with UCCA, and its stability, assessing UCCA's influence on commonly studied structural divergences.

4.1 Portability

We examine UCCA's applicability to French by systematically examining the major grammatical phenomena in French, and verifying that UCCA categories can be applied to them. To this purpose, we use the same annotation guidelines and category set previously applied to English, and apply it to the phenomena and examples described in a French grammar book (Hawkins and Towell, 2001). Tense and agreement are not covered in the UCCA foundational layer which we use, and are therefore disregarded in this work.

We find that even for French-specific phenomena, current UCCA categories permit their annotation in the foundational layer without requiring changes in the definitions or additional categories. Due to space limitations, we only present here one case of interest. The full analysis according to the grammar book can be found in Sulem (2014) (Appendix 2) [3].

As an example, we consider reflexive pronouns, representing the applicability of UCCA to French phenomena that have no direct parallel in English. In French, in addition to the counterparts of "himself" and "themselves" ("lui-même" and "eux-mêmes"), reflexivity is also expressed through the pronouns "se", "me", "te", "nous" and "vous", which precede some verbs (termed "pronominal verbs"). For instance, "lavé" is "washed", while "s'est lavé" is "washed himself". We show that the UCCA's category definitions can be applied naturally to this phenomenon.

A key guideline in UCCA is that the annotation of a unit does not depend on its part of speech but rather on its meaning and role in the context it is situated in. We therefore distinguish between three cases based on their semantics.

First, cases where the reflexive pronoun refers to the same Participant as the subject. Here the pronoun is annotated as an A: "[Jean]$_A$ [s']$_A$ [est lavé]$_P$" ("Jean washed himself").

Second, cases where the pronoun changes the meaning of the verb in an unpredictable way, or alternatively, where the verb may only appear in a pronominal form. In these cases the formal means of reflexivity is used, but is not associated with the semantic phenomena of reflexivity. Semantically then, the reflexive pronoun and the verb form one unanalyzable unit, as in the following example: "Il [s' est aperçu]$_P$ qu'il était tard" ("He realized that it was late").

Third, cases where the pronoun changes the meaning and the number of arguments of the verb without creating semantic reflexivity. In these cases the verb is the Center (C) of the Process, while the reflexive pronoun serves as an Elaborator (E). For example: "Je [m'$_E$ appelle$_C$]$_P$ John" ("my name is John" where "appelle" means "call").

4.2 Stability

Overcoming cross-linguistic divergences (or translation divergences) is one of the main challenges in machine translation. We briefly review the main examples of translation divergences presented in (Dorr, 1994; Dorr et al., 2002; Dorr et al., 2004), adapting the original English-Spanish examples to English-French analogues. Then, for each example, we present its annotation according

[3]www.cs.huji.ac.il/~eliors/papers/elior_sulem_thesis.pdf

to UCCA. The resulting annotations show that UCCA abstracts away from almost all of these divergences and exposes the semantic similarity, demonstrating the stability of the scheme at the type-level.

Categorical divergence: Translation of words in one language into words that have different POS tags in another language. For example, "to be cold" – "avoir froid" ("to have cold"). In UCCA the expression in both languages is annotated as a State where the Center (similar to the notion of a semantic head) is "cold" / "froid".

Conflational divergence: Translation of two or more words in one language into one word in another language. For example: "to kick" – "donner un coup de pied" ("give a kick"). In UCCA, the expression describes a Process in the two languages, and the French light verb "donner" ("give") is a Function (a unit which does not introduce a relation or participant) inside the Process.

Structural[4] divergence: Realization of verb arguments in different syntactic configurations in different languages. For example, "to enter the house" – "entrer dans la maison" ("enter in the house"). In UCCA there is a Participant in both languages.

Thematic divergence: Realization of verb arguments in syntactic configurations that reflect different thematic to syntactic mapping orders. For example, "I like this house" – "Cette maison me plaît" ("this house pleases to me"). In UCCA there are two Participants in English as well as two Participants in French ("cette maison" / "this house" and "me" / "me").

Promotional/Demotional divergence: Promotion is the case where a modifier in the source language is promoted to a main verb in the target language (Dorr, 1990; Gola, 2012). Demotion is its mirror image, where a main verb in the source language becomes a modifier in the target language.

An example where an English adverb is promoted to a main verb is the French: "John usually goes home" – "John a l'habitude de rentrer à la maison" ("John has the habit to go home"). In UCCA, both "usually" and "a l'habitude" ("has the habit") are annotated as Adverbials.

An example where an English verb is demoted to an adverb is the French "to run in" – "entrer en courant" ("enter running"). In UCCA, the English example contains a Process ("to run") and a Participant ("in"). The annotation in French is somewhat different, where "entrer" ("enter") is a Process, while "en courant" ("running") is an Adverbial.

To summarize, aside from the case of demotional divergence, the UCCA annotation (in its foundational layer) abstracts away from canonical examples for cross-linguistic divergences. With demotional divergence, where UCCA annotation is different across languages, we note that the divergence does correspond to a semantic difference of emphasis, that is, whether the entering action or the running action is the main relation. We leave it open whether this divergence should be considered a result of a true semantic difference between the languages or a shortcoming of UCCA that fails to capture the similarity between them.

5 Parallel French-English UCCA Corpus

The parallel corpus. The French-English corpus used here is an extract from the book *Twenty Thousand Leagues Under the Sea* (*Vingt Mille Lieues Sous les Mers*), a classic science fiction novel written in French by Jules Verne (1828–1905) and first published in 1870. We use an online version of the book and the English translation by J.P. Walter (Verne, 1870; Verne, 1991). Each of the two monolingual parts of the corpus contain 583 sentences which correspond to 12.5K tokens in English and 13.1K tokens in French. The annotated corpus is publically available[5].

Initial alignment. We segment the parallel corpus into 154 bilingual pairs of aligned passages. Each passage in French corresponds to a single passage in English. The passages correspond to the paragraphs in the original texts except in a few cases of long dialogues, where we split the paragraphs into several passages. A sentence-level alignment is not necessary in our analysis since in UCCA, the text is viewed as a collection of Scenes, where sentence boundaries play no significant role.

Manual annotation. The annotation was carried out using UCCA's web application. Both French and English texts were annotated by the same annotator (one of the authors of the paper), according to UCCA annotation guidelines[6]. Re-

[4] Here the term "structural" refers specifically to syntax, in contrast to the broader sense used elsewhere in the paper.

[5] www.cs.huji.ac.il/~eliors

[6] Both the web-application and the guidelines are available in homepages.inf.ed.ac.uk/oabend/ucca/.

cent updates to the guidelines concerning the annotation of secondary verbs as Adverbials, are not applied here. We expect these changes to further improve the quality of the results (Section 7.3). The annotation in English and French was carried out separately in each of the languages, rather than in parallel, thus permitting cases where the same linguistic form in English and French is subject to different interpretations, leading to different annotations. This effect on the differences in UCCA annotation in English and French is discussed in Section 7.

6 Token-level Analysis

In order to demonstrate UCCA's stability at a token-level, we examine the number of UCCA units of various types in both English and French for each parallel passage in our annotated parallel corpus. We compare these numbers to those obtained through syntactic annotation. In light of our type-level analysis (Section 4), we expect these UCCA categories to be more stable cross-linguistically than syntactic ones. The number of Scenes is compared to the number of non-auxiliary verbs, and the number of Participants and Adverbials is compared to the number of noun phrases (NPs), prepositional phrases (PPs) and adverb phrases (ADVPs).

We note that English-French is a particularly challenging candidate for this type of analysis since the language pair is relatively structurally similar (e.g., measured by word reordering (Birch, 2011)). Syntactic annotation is therefore a strong baseline. We expect UCCA's relative stability to be even greater in more syntactically divergent language pairs.

We are mainly interested not in the absolute number of units/constituents of a certain type, but more in the extent to which this number diverges between languages. Minimal divergence in the number of units/constituents of a certain type between the two languages is an indication of the scheme's stability.

We compute the similarity in the number of units/constituents of each type in the two languages in the following manner. For each language $l \in \{Fre, Eng\}$ and for each unit/constituent type t, we compute the number of instances of that type $n_i^{(t,l)}$ in each passage $i = 1, .., N$. We thereby obtain for each (t, l) a vector $n^{(t,l)} = \{n_i^{(t,l)}\}_i$. For each type t, the similarity between $n^{(t,Fre)}$ and $n^{(t,Eng)}$, which is an indication of the stability of the scheme, is computed using l_1 and l_2 norms of the difference between them.

We further compute an F-score as follows: precision and recall of the French vector against the English one are defined respectively by $P = s/f$ and $R = s/e$ when $s = \sum_i \min(n_i^{(t,Fre)}, n_i^{(t,Eng)})$, $f = \sum_i n_i^{(t,Fre)}$ and $e = \sum_i n_i^{(t,Eng)}$. The F-score F is the harmonic mean of P and R. This measure provides an upper bound of the number of aligned units in the two languages, looking at the category of the units and their appearance in aligned passages. We note that the measures described are more applicable in this context than statistical correlation measures (e.g., the Pearson correlation coefficient). This is because a stable scheme is determined by the similarity of the count vectors in absolute terms, rather than their statistical correlation.

Experimental setup. For tagging, we use the Stanford POS tagger package (Toutanova et al., 2003). We compute the number of verbs in the parallel corpus and compare them to the number of Scenes. We exclude auxiliaries since such verbs tend to differ considerably between languages. We manually correct the tagging (by a single annotator, highly proficient in both languages), and therefore expect these numbers to be comparable in quality to a gold standard[7].

The syntactic constituents we study are noun phrases (*NP*), prepositional phrases (*PP*) and adverb phrases (*ADVP* in English and *AdP* in French). We used the Stanford parser's pre-trained models for English (*englishPCFG*, (Klein and Manning, 2003)) and French (the *frenchFactored* (Green et al., 2011)), with the same manual tokenization taken from the UCCA annotation. Six passages which contain very long sentences in French and for which the parser was unable to produce a parse were omitted from this evaluation. We note that we include in our analysis Scenes marked as unanalyzable (For example: "Hello!"), but exclude Scenes appearing as remote Participants, so to avoid double counting.

In order to correct for possible biases of the parsers towards overprediction or underprediction of certain syntactic constituents, we conduct the following experiment. We manually count the

[7]The French tagger overestimated the number of verbs by 0.6%, while the English tagger overestimated it by 8.7%.

	l_1	l_2	F	Fr. Avg.	En. Avg.
Scenes	**124**	**14.97**	**0.96**	9.25	9.49
Verbs	157	18.79	0.94	9.30	9.10
Participants (As)	**273**	**31.13**	**0.95**	17.68	18.27
NPs and PPs	952	102.74	0.89	26.64	32.33
NPs	847	88.89	0.87	18.78	24.20
PPs	299	32.05	0.87	7.86	8.13
Adverbials (Ds)	**133**	**17.18**	**0.86**	3.3	3.07
Adverb Phrases	342	40.0	0.15	0.24	2.49
As + Ds	**334**	**37.18**	**0.95**	20.99	21.34
NPs+PPs+ADVPs	1226	127.40	0.87	26.88	34.82

Table 1: Comparison of UCCA's Scene, Participant and Adverbial stability across the two languages with the stability of verbs, NPs, PPs and ADVPs. l_1 and l_2 represent respectively the l1 and l2 norms of the difference between the French and English count vectors. The F-score F, resulting from an upper bound on the number of aligned units in the two languages, evaluates the similarity between these vectors. The Scenes and the verbs are computed over the whole corpus (154 passages), while the other categories are computed on 148 passages (see text).

number of NPs, PPs and ADVPs in the first 10 passages in English and French, according to the original guidelines of the English and French Treebanks (Bies et al., 1995; Abeillé et al., 2004). All borderline cases are counted pessimistically, i.e., in the direction that maximizes the difference between the manual and automatic counts.

Results. Our results are given in Table 1. In all cases the UCCA annotation is more stable across annotations than the syntactic counterpart. The relative similarity between the number of PPs in the two languages, as reflected in the relatively low vector distances of $n^{(PP,Eng)}$ and $n^{(PP,Fre)}$, can be explained by the fact that the presence of a preposition in French usually requires a preposition in its English translation. PPs are also less affected than NPs by nominalizations which often result in cross-linguistic syntactic divergences[8]. Table 1 also presents the average number of units/constituents of each type per passage, on the two right columns. The latter numbers cannot be seen as a measure of stability, as an excessive number of units in one passage (relative to the translation) may cancel out a deficient number of units in another.

Concerning the correction term for the parsers' biases, we find that in the first 10 passages, the English parser overpredicted NPs by 12.2% and underpredicted ADVPs by 3.8%. The same number of English PPs was obtained through manual and automatic counting. In these passages the French parser overpredicted NPs by 0.9% and PPs by 11.4%. The average difference between the results of the manual and automatic counting of French adverb phrases was 0.5. The biases are in an order of magnitude less than the relative differences in the l_1 and l_2 norms. Therefore, the stability of UCCA relative to syntactic schemes is not a result of the parsers' biases.

7 Divergence Analysis and Discussion

The analysis in Section 6 provides a comparison in terms of the number of units of specific types, as opposed to corresponding numbers of syntactic constituents. In this section we define a more refined methodology (Section 7.1) for examining not only the correspondence in the number of units between the languages, but also the semantic correspondence between units (Section 7.2 and 7.3).

7.1 Defining Divergences using UCCA

We define a *correspondence* between two UCCA annotations to be a one-to-one mapping which preserves UCCA's categories and meaning. Concretely, given a parallel corpus, a unit in one language corresponds to a unit in the other language if they have the same category and if the units have the same meaning. More formally, we define a *sufficient subset* of a unit u to be a subset of e that contains its heads (the main relation in the case of a Scene, or the Centers in the case of a non-Scene). For example, "He ran" is a sufficient subset of the Scene "He slowly ran" since it contains the main relation "ran". A unit e in English and a unit f in French correspond to each other if they have the same category and any of the three following conditions hold: (1) e is a translation of f, (2) a sufficient subset of e is a translation of f, or (3) a sufficient subset of f is a translation of e. For example, the English Scene "He slowly ran" corresponds to the French Scene "Il a couru" ("He ran") since condition (2) holds.

Given a UCCA category, some of the units of that category are left unaligned between the two sides of the parallel corpus, creating a *UCCA divergence*. We classify UCCA divergences according to their category, defining Scene, Participant and Adverbial divergences. We distinguish between divergences in the English and French sides.

An example of a UCCA divergence from our French-English corpus is: "of the ship victimized by this new ramming" – "du navire victime de ce

[8]The low number of French adverb phrases is partially due to the presence of some adverbial expressions that were tagged as multi-word adverbs (MWADV). If we consider MWADV as adverb phrases as well, the l_1 value is 292 and the l_2 value is 33.05, which is still much higher than the distances for UCCA's Adverbials (133 for l_1 and 17.18 for l_2).

	Property	Scene Div.		Participant Div.		Adverbial Div.	
		Eng.	Fre.	Eng.	Fre.	Eng.	Fre.
	Translation Study						
1	Similar Translation Possible	65.18	58.33	50	35.29	70.83	50.0
2	Similar Source Possible	73.21	63.89	54.55	47.06	75.0	46.15
-	None	18.75	31.94	38.64	47.06	16.67	42.31
	Annotation Study						
3	Conforming Analysis	41.96	54.16	72.72	73.53	25.0	53.85
4	Different Interpretation	10.71	1.39	25	23.53	8.33	7.69
–	None	55.36	44.44	25	20.59	70.83	46.15
	Semantic Effect of the Unaligned Unit						
5	Additional Information	38.39	18.06	25.0	20.59	37.50	0.0
6	Tense Information	8.04	5.56	–	–	–	–
7	Emphasis	19.64	8.33	31.82	26.47	41.67	3.85
–	None	50.89	80.56	61.36	64.71	58.33	96.15

Table 2: Percentage of UCCA divergences according to their types (columns) that have certain properties (rows). All numbers are percentages computed over all UCCA divergences of the given type. Note that the properties are not mutually exclusive (see text). Participant and Adverbial divergences are only evaluated on passages with no Scene divergences.

nouvel abordage". The French noun "victime" describes a result, while the corresponding English "victimized" is an action. The unaligned Scene is in English. It is therefore an *English Scene divergence*. In the example "He slowly ran"/"Il a couru" we saw above, there is no Scene divergences but the English Adverbial "slowly" is unaligned, creating an *English Adverbial divergence*.

7.2 Number of UCCA Divergences

The analysis of Scene divergences is performed manually over the entire set of passages. The analysis of Participant and Adverbial divergences is restricted to passages with no Scene divergences, i.e., with a perfect Scene to Scene correspondence (57 passages of the total 154). This permits the capture of lower level divergences which are not just consequences of the divergences at the Scene level.

We found a total of 112 English Scene divergences and 72 French ones. This amounted to 92.3% of the English Scenes having a French correspondent and 94.9% of the French Scenes having an English correspondent. Only 25% of the sentences (148 out of 583) contains any Scene divergences.

Concerning Participant divergences, we found that 694 out of 738 English Participants (94.0%) have a correspondent in French. 694 of the 728 French Participants (95.3%) have a correspondent in English. 100 out of the 124 English Adverbials (80.6%) have a correspondent in French, and 100 out of the 126 Adverbials (79.4%) have a correspondent in English. Thus, our results show low rates of UCCA French-English divergences.

We also conduct a preliminary study into the applicability of another semantic scheme, namely AMR, to our domain. We annotate 10 sentence pairs with AMR. Our analysis shows that AMR conserves the main structures in most sentences (7 out of 10), and suggests that other semantic annotations may also be structurally stable. However, semantic roles, used in PropBank and AMR, are often a source of divergences across the languages.

7.3 Properties of UCCA Divergences

In order to examine the causes and semantic types of the different divergences, we manually classified each of them according to three groups of properties, which are not mutually exclusive. The results of the divergence analysis are presented in Table 2.

Translation study: The properties in this group investigate whether a given UCCA divergence can be avoided using a different formulation closer to the one used in the other language. This approach evaluates the translator's choices and creativity. Properties #1 and #2 check whether different formulations can be used in the source and target side respectively, that would avoid the UCCA divergence. Results show that many of the divergences can be indeed ascribed to the specific translation selected. For example, only less than a third of the Scene divergences in each language could not have been avoided through a different translation. We thus speculate that in a more technical and less literary corpus, the number of UCCA divergences will be lower.

Annotation study: These properties study the influence of the annotator's preferences. Property #3 (conforming analysis) covers cases where UCCA allows another analysis which would have avoided the divergence. While both annotations are permitted, one of them is sometimes preferred, to capture a nuance of meaning conveyed by one language but not the other. Property #4 refers to

Replaced by	Scene Div.		Participant Div.		Adverbial Div.	
	Eng.	Fre.	Eng.	Fre.	Eng.	Fre.
Linker	6.25	1.39	–	–	8.33	7.69
Ground	1.79	1.39	–	–	4.17	3.85
Elaborator of Participant	–	–	0	2.94	4.17	19.23
Main Relation	–	–	20.45*	20.59*	25.0*	26.92*
Parallel Scene	–	–	13.64	2.94	–	–
Participant	–	–	–	–	4.17	11.54
Adverbial	–	–	6.82	2.94	–	–
2 Participants	–	–	11.36	2.94	–	–
2 Adverbials	–	–	–	–	4.17	0.0
None	91.96	98.21	47.73	67.65	50.0	30.77

Table 3: Analysis of divergences in terms of replacements by other UCCA categories. Columns correspond to divergence types, while rows correspond to the category, as defined in Abend and Rappoport (2013b), of the replacing unit. All numbers are given in percents. Percentage is taken over all UCCA divergences of the same type. *: In these cases, a Participant or an Adverbial in one of the languages is included in the meaning of the main relation (Process or State) in the other language.

divergences resulting from different readings (ambiguity) allowed by the text, where one meaning was selected in one language and another in the other. The results for this group (properties #3 and #4) reveal that most of the Scene and Adverbial divergences could have been avoided had a different annotation been selected. This suggests that more restrictive annotation guidelines or some post-annotation normalization can substantially reduce the number of divergences.

Effect of the unaligned unit: Divergences are often a result of a semantic or pragmatic difference between the source text and its translation. Property #5 addresses cases where additional information is conveyed by the unaligned unit. Property #6 is a sub-case of #5 that specifically addresses tense information. Property #7 addresses cases where the unaligned unit emphasizes some aspect of meaning. The results show that many divergences can be ascribed to a true semantic difference between the source and the translation.

Finally, in some cases, the UCCA divergences simply replace one UCCA category with another (Table 3). In these cases there are unaligned units in the English and the French sides that roughly correspond to one another semantically, but have different UCCA categories. Cases of replacement are common with Participant and Adverbial divergences, but fairly rare in the case of Scene divergences. In case of Adverbial divergences, many of them result from including the meaning of an Adverbial in one language in the meaning of the main relation (Process or State) in the other language. This can be seen as a generalization of demotional/promotional divergences (Dorr, 1994) discussed in Section 4.2. Annotating secondary verbs (e.g., "begin" or "try") as Adverbials instead of being part of the main relation, as was done in the latest version of UCCA's guidelines, may considerably reduce this kind of divergence.

To summarize, our study sheds light on the circumstances in which UCCA divergences arise and suggests how many divergences can be avoided. This study also contributes to the understanding of the differences between original and translated texts, which can improve MT (Lembersky et al., 2013).

8 Conclusion

We showed that basic semantic structures can be stably preserved across English-French translations. This means that semantic structures may be more suitable to SMT systems than syntactic ones, which exhibit well known divergence phenomena. We used the UCCA scheme, but we expect these advantages to generalize to other structured semantic schemes. Future work will address the integration of UCCA into structure-based SMT either by adding UCCA as features to phrase-based and syntax-based systems, or by replacing existing syntactic structures with UCCA structures. We also plan to investigate related tasks that would benefit from UCCA's stability like bilingual alignment and MT evaluation.

Acknowledgments

We would like to thank Roy Schwartz for helpful comments. This research was supported by the Language, Logic and Cognition Center (LLCC) at the Hebrew University of Jerusalem (for the first author) and by the ERC Advanced Fellowship 249520 GRAMPLUS (for the second author).

References

Anne Abeillé, François Toussenel, and Martine Chéradame, 2004. *Corpus le Monde Annotation en constituents Guide pour les cor-*

recteurs. http://www.llf.cnrs.fr/Gens/Abeille/guide-annot.pdf.

Omri Abend and Ari Rappoport. 2013a. UCCA: A semantic-based grammatical annotation scheme. In *Proc. of IWCS-13*, pages 1–12.

Omri Abend and Ari Rappoport. 2013b. Universal Conceptual Cognitive Annotation (UCCA). In *Proc. of ACL-13*, pages 228–238.

Collin F. Baker, Charles J. Fillmore, and John B. Lowe. 1998. The Berkeley Framenet project. In *Proc. of ACL-COLING-98*, pages 86–90.

Laura Banarescu, Claire Bonial, Shu Cai, Madalina Georgescu, Kira Griffitt, Ulf Hermjakob, Kevin Knight, Philipp Koehn, Martha Palmer, and Nathan Schneider. 2013. Abstract Meaning Representation for sembanking. In *Proc. of Linguistic Annotation Workshop and Interoperability with Discourse*, pages 178–186.

Mazrieh Bazrafshan and Daniel Gildea. 2013. Semantic roles for string to tree machine translation. In *Proc. of ACL-13 (Short Paper)*, pages 419–423.

Ann Bies, Mark Ferguson, Karen Katz, and Robert MacIntyre, 1995. *Bracketting Guidelines for Treebank II Style Penn Treebank Project*. Linguistic Data Consortium.

Alexandra Birch, Barry Haddow, Ulrich Germann, Maria Nadejde, Chrsitian Buck, and Philipp Koehn. 2013. The feasibility of HMEANT as a human MT evaluation metric. In *Proc. of the 8th Workshop on SMT, ACL-13*, pages 52–61.

Alexandra Birch. 2011. *Reordering metrics for statistical machine translation*. Ph.D. thesis, University of Edinburgh.

Aljoscha Burchardt, Katrin Erk, Anette Frank, Andrea Kowalski, Sebastian Padó, and Manfred Pinkal. 2009. Using FrameNet for the semantic analysis of German: Annotation, representation and automation. In Hans C. Boas (Herausgeber), editor, *Multilingual FrameNets in Computational Lexicography - Methods and Applications*, pages 209–244, New York/Berlin. Mouton de Gruyter.

David Chiang. 2005. A hierarchical phrase-based model for statistical machine translation. In *Proc. of ACL-05*, pages 263–270.

Yuan Ding and Martha Palmer. 2004. Synchronous dependency insertion grammars: a grammar formalism for syntax based statistical MT. In *Workshop on Recent Advances in Dependency Grammars, COLING-04*.

Robert M.W. Dixon. 2010a. *Basic Linguistic Theory: Grammatical Topics*, volume 2. Oxford University Press.

Robert M.W. Dixon. 2010b. *Basic Linguistic Theory: Methodology*, volume 1. Oxford University Press.

Robert M.W. Dixon. 2012. *Basic Linguistic Theory: Further Grammatical Topics*, volume 3. Oxford University Press.

Bonnie J. Dorr, Lisa Pearl, Rebecca Hwa, and Nizard Habash. 2002. DUSTer: a method for unraveling cross-language divergences for statistical word-level alignment. In *Proc.of AMTA-02*, pages 31–43.

Bonnie J. Dorr, Eduard H. Hovy, and Lori S. Levin. 2004. Machine translation: interlingual methods. In *Encyclopedia of language and linguistics, 2nd edition*. ms.939, Brown, Keith.

Bonnie Dorr, Rebecca Passonneau, David Farwell, Rebecca Green, Nizar Habash, Stephen Helmreich, Edward Hovy, Lori Levin, Keith Miller, Teruko Mitamura, Owen Rambow, and Advaith Siddharthan. 2010. Interlingual annotation of parallel text corpora: A new framework for annotation and evaluation. *Natural Language Engineering*, pages 197–243.

Bonnie Dorr. 1990. Solving thematic divergences in machine translation. In *Proc. of ACL-90*, pages 127–134.

Bonnie J. Dorr. 1994. Machine translation divergences: a formal description and proposed solution. *Computational linguistics*, 20(4):597–635.

Shimon Edelman and Zach Solan. 2009. Machine translation using automatically inferred construction-based correspondence and language models. In *Proc. of PACLIC-09*, pages 654–661.

Minwei Feng, Wiwei Sun, and Hermann Ney. 2012. Semantic cohesion model for phrase-based SMT. *Proc. of COLING-12*, pages 867–878.

Jeffrey Flanigan, Sam Thomson, Jaime Carbonell, Chris Dyer, and Noah A. Smith. 2014. A discriminative graph-based parser for the Abstract Meaning Representation. In *Proc. of ACL-14*, pages 1426–1436.

Pascale Fung, Zhojun Wu, Yongsheng Yang, and Dekai Wu. 2006. Learning of Chinese/English semantic structure mapping. In *Workshop on Spoken Language Technology, IEEE/ACL-06*, pages 230–233.

Pascale Fung, Zhaojun Wu, Yongsheng Yang, and Dekai Wu. 2007. Learning bilingual semantic frames: shallow semantic parsing vs. semantic role projection. In *Proc. of the 11th Conference on Theoretical and Methodological Issues in Machine Translation (TMI 2007)*, pages 75–84.

Francesca Gola. 2012. An analysis of translation divergence patterns using PanLex translation pairs. Master's thesis, University of Washington.

Spence Green, Marie-Catherine de Marneffe, John Bauer, and Christopher D. Manning. 2011. Multiword expression identification with Tree Substitution Grammars: a parsing tour de force with French. In *Proc. of EMNLP-11*, pages 725–735.

Roger Hawkins and Richard Towell. 2001. *French Grammar and Usage*. McGraw-Hill, 2nd edition.

Bevan Jones, Jacob Andreas, Daniel Bauer, Karl Moritz Hermann, and Kevin Knight. 2012. Semantics-based machine translation with hyperedge replacement grammars. In *Proc. of COLING-12*, pages 1359–1376.

Dan Klein and Christopher D. Manning. 2003. Accurate unlexicalized parsing. In *Proc. of ACL-03*, pages 423–430.

Mikhail Kozhevnikov and Ivan Titov. 2013. Cross-lingual transfer of semantic role labeling models. In *Proc. of ACL-13*, pages 1190–1200.

Ronald W. Langacker. 2008. *Cognitive Grammar: A Basic Introduction*. Oxford University Press, USA.

Gennadi Lembersky, Noam Ordan, and Shuly Wintner. 2013. Improving statistical machine translation by adapting translation models to translationese. *Computational Linguistics*, 39(4):999–1023.

Mike Lewis and Mark Steedman. 2013. Unsupervised induction of cross-lingual semantic relations. In *Proc. of EMNLP-13*, pages 681–692.

Junhui Li, Philip Resnik, and Hal Daumé III. 2013. Modeling syntactic and semantic structures in hierarchical phrase-based translation. In *Proc. of NAACL-HLT-13*, pages 540–549.

Ding Liu and Daniel Gildea. 2010. Semantic role features for machine translation. In *Proc. of COLING-10*, pages 716–724.

Yang Liu, Qun Liu, and Shouxun Lin. 2006. Tree-to-string alignment template for statistical machine translation. In *Proc. of COLING-ACL-06*, pages 609–616.

Daniel Marcu, Wei Wang, Abdessamad Echihabi, and Kevin Knight. 2006. SPMT: Statistical machine translation with syntactified target language phrases. In *Proc. of EMNLP-06*, pages 44–52.

Haitao Mi, Liang Huang, and Qun Liu. 2008. Forest-based translation. In *Proc. of ACL-08 HLT*, pages 192–199.

Sergei Nirenburg. 1989. New developments in knowledge-based machine translation. In Alatis J.E., editor, *Georgetown University Round Table on Languages and Linguistics 1989: Language teaching, testing, and technology: lessons from the past with a view toward the future*, pages 344–357. Georgetown University Press.

Martha Palmer, Daniel Gildea, and Paul Kingsbury. 2005. The proposition bank: A annotated corpus of semantic roles. *Computational Linguistics*, 31(1):149–159.

Tanja Samardžić, Lonneke van der Plas, Goljihan Kashaeva, and Paola Merlo. 2010a. The scope and the sources of variation in verbal predicates in English and French. In *Proc. of the 9th International Workshop on Treebanks and Linguistic Theories*, pages 199–211.

Tanja Samardžić, Lonneke van der Plas, Goljihan Kashaeva, and Paola Merlo. 2010b. Variation in verbal predicates in English and French. *Generative Grammar in Geneva*, 6:109–135.

Elior Sulem. 2014. Integration of a cognitive annotation into machine translation: Theoretical foundations and bilingual corpus analysis. Master's thesis, Hebrew University of Jerusalem.

Kristina Toutanova, Dan Klein, Christopher Manning, and Yoram Singer. 2003. Feature-rich part-of-speech tagging with a cyclic dependency network. In *Proc. of HLT-NAACL-03*, pages 252–259.

Hiroshi Uchida. 1987. ATLAS: Fujitsu machine translation system. In *Machine Translation Summit*, Japan.

Zdeňka Urešová, Ondřej Dušek, Eva Fučíková, Jan Hajič, and Jana Šindlerová. 2015. Bilingual English-Czech valency lexicon linked to a parallel corpus. In *Proc. of the 9th Linguistic Annotation Workshop (The LAW IX)*, pages 124–128.

Lonneke van der Plas, Tanja Samardžić, and Paola Merlo. 2010. Cross-lingual validity of PropBank in the manual annotation of French. In *Proc. of the 4th Linguistic Annotation Workshop (The LAW IV)*, pages 113–117.

Jules Verne. 1870. *Vingt Mille Lieues Sous les Mers*. J. Hetzel. `http://fr.wikisource.org/wiki/Vingt_mille_lieues_sous_les_mers`.

Jules Verne. 1991. Twenty Thousands Leagues Under the Sea. Translated from the original French by J.P. Walter. `http://jv.gilead.org.il/fpwalter`.

Ralph Weischedel, Sameer Pradhan, Lance Ramshaw, Jeff Kaufman, Michelle Franchini, Mohammed El-Bachouti, Nianwen Xue, Martha Palmer, Jena D. Hwang, Claire Bonial, Jinho Choi, Aous Mansouri, Maha Foster, Abdel aati Hawwary, Mitchell Marcus, Ann Taylor, Craig Greenberg, Eduard Hovy, Robert Belvin, and Ann Houston. 2012. OntoNotes Release 5.0. Technical report, Linguistic Data Consortium 2013T19.

Dekai Wu and Pascale Fung. 2009. Semantic roles for SMT: a hybrid two-pass model. In *Proc. of NAACL-HLT-09 (Short Paper)*, pages 13–19.

Deyi Xiong, Min Zhang, and Haizhou Li. 2012. Modeling the translation of predicate-argument structure for SMT. In *Proc. of ACL-12*, pages 902–911.

Nianwen Xue, Ondřej Bojar, Jan Hajič, Martha Palmer, Zdeňka Urešová, and Xiuhong Zhang. 2014. Not an interlingua, but close: comparison of English AMRs to Chinese and Czech. In *Proc. of LREC-14*, pages 1765–1772.

Feifei Zhai, Jiajun Zhang, Yu Zhou, and Chengquing Zong. 2012. Machine translation by modeling predicate-argument structure transformation. In *Proc. of COLING-12*, pages 3019–3036.

Min Zhang, Hongfei Jiang, Aiti Aw, Haizhou Li, Chew Lim Tan, and Seng Li. 2008. A tree sequence alignment-based tree-to-tree translation model. In *Proc. of ACL-08*, pages 559–567.

Integrating Case Frame into Japanese to Chinese Hierarchical Phrase-based Translation Model

JinAn Xu, JiangMing Liu, YuFeng Chen, YuJie Zhang, Fang Ming and Shaotong Li
Beijing Key Lab of Traffic Data Analysis and Mining
School of Computer and Information Technology, Beijing Jiaotong University
Haidian District, Beijing, China
{jaxu,12120432,chenyf,yjzhang,14120416,11281094}@bjtu.edu.cn

Abstract

This paper presents a novel approach to enhance hierarchical phrase-based (HP-B) machine translation systems with case frame (CF).we integrate the Japanese shallow CF into both rule extraction and decoding. All of these rules are then employed to decode new sentences in Japanese with source language case frame. The results of experiments carried out on Japanese-Chinese test sets. It shows that our approach maintains the advantages of HPB translation systems while at the same time naturally incorporates CF constraints. The case frame rules can complement Hiero-style rules. Our approach is especially effective for language pairs with large word order differences, such as Japanese-to-Chinese.

1 Introduction

In the Japanese-Chinese machine translation task, reordering is the main problem due to substantial differences in sentence structures between these two languages. For example, Japanese has a subject-object-verb (SOV) structure, while, Chinese has a subject-verb-object (SVO) structure.

The pre-ordering technology is one way to handle this problem (Wu, et al., 2011), but it needs to train a pre-ordering model. An hierarchical phrase-based (HPB) model (Chiang, 2005; Chiang, 2007) is a powerful method to cover any format of translation pairs by using synchronous context free grammar. Hiero grammars can capture complex nested translation relationships to handle reordering. However, due to its compromise on the efficiency of rule extraction and decoding, (a) a source language span limit is applied with 10, (b) the number of non-terminals in one rule is set to 2, (c) there is a prohibition of consecutive non-terminals on the source language side of a rule and (d) coarse-grained rules. The HPB model does not perform well when reordering in a Japanese-Chinese machine translation task as shown in Figure 1, which shows an example of long distance reordering covering 13 words.

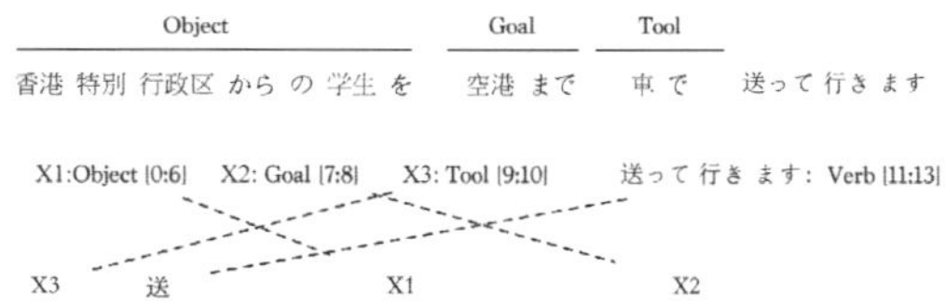

Figure 1: The reordering problem in Japanese-Chinese translation

With a traditional approach, the typical H-PB model fails to capture complex reordering information as shown in Figure 1. By contrast, Fillmore (1968) has proposed case grammar, which is effectively proved and originally used in rule-based machine translation (RBMT) system (Yamabana,1997). Furthermore, Kawahara (1994, 2002) defines the Japanese shallow CF that is widely and successfully used in Japanese dependency tasks provided by CoNLL-09 (Hajič, 2011). Figure 2 shows the CF's ability to capture reordering information.

In this paper, we describe effective approaches to introducing source language Japanese CF in the Japanese-Chinese translation task. Unlike previous work, we are the first to use Japanese CF information on the HPB model, and to transform CF information into SCFG style rules, which is suitable and useful in the original HPB decoder. By importing CF into the HPB model, we expand search space and introduce fine-grained rules.

The remainder of this paper is organized as follows. After introducing Japanese CF,the proposed approach is introduced in Section 3; the experimental results and associate analysis are given

Proceedings of the 1st Workshop on Semantics-Driven Statistical Machine Translation, pages 23–29,
Beijing, China, July 30, 2015.

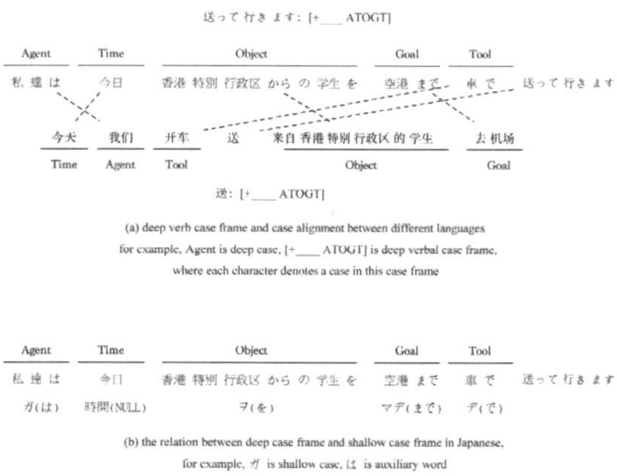

Figure 2: Deep verbal CF and shallow verbal case between Japanese and Chinese

in Section 4. Section 5 briefly discusses related work; Finally, conclusions are drawn in Section 6.

2 Case Frame

Unlike HPB model's format grammar, case grammar is linguistically sensible and is applied to semantically analyze sentence. Based on case grammar, a sentence will be analyzed using different deep case components (agent, instrument, experiencer, object, location, benefactive, factitive, goal, source and time). This way, Fillmore has defined the deep verb CF, where one example is shown in Figure 2(a).

Deep case is language independent. If two sentences from different languages have the exactly same meaning and description, they will have the same deep case grammar analysis. Figure 2(a) shows the sentence "today we will get him to the airport by car" described respectively in Japanese and Chinese. Meanwhile, Figure 2(a) shows deep case alignment between these two different languages. Deep case alignment in two different languages is one to one mapping. For example, in Figure 2(a), "私 達 は" (we) is the agent in Japanese, mapping " 我们 " (we) (agent) in Chinese.

The deep CF is well known, but it is rarely used in statistical machine translation due to the difficulty of the auto-analysis for all languages including Japanese. However, due to the explicit case in Japanese, Kawahara (2002) redefines the shallow verbal CF in Japanese shown in Figure 2(b), where an auxiliary word contributes to the shallow CF analysis. As a result, recent research has achieved high accuracy (more than 90%) on Japanese shallow CF analysis (Kawahara and Kurohashi, 2006). Between the deep case and the Japanese shallow case, there is a many-to-many relation shown in Table 1. In this paper, we will only use "case frame" to represent Japanese verbal shallow CF for short.

Type	Examples of Japanese shallow case
Agent	ガ (ga)
Object	ニ(ni), ヘ(he), ヲ(wo)
Instrument	ニ(ni), デ(de)
Experiencer	ニ(ni), ト(to), ヘ(he)
Source	ニ(ni), ヘ(he), カラ(kara), ヨリ(uori) マデ(made), ノ(no)
Goal	ニ(ni), ヘ(he)
Location	ニ(ni), デ(de), カラ(kara) ヨリ(yori), マデ(made)
Time	ニ(ni), デ(de), カラ(kara) ヨリ(yori), マデ(made)
Others	無格(none), 修飾(modification)

Table 1: The mapping between a deep case and a Japanese shallow case.

3 The proposed approach

A case frame is the linguistic concept, which provides linguistic guidance for derivation. Here, we present a method to alleviate complex reordering problems in the Japanese-Chinese machine translation task with case frame.

Generally, we obtain both the case frame and the hiero-style SCFG from the training data, and then transfer the case frame rule (CFR) to SCFG style and use both of them in decoding with the SCFG. The method benefits from both hiero-style translation and linguistic information. In the rule extraction of our approach, we acquire case frame rules using fuzzy strategy and hiero-style rules using traditional HPB rule extraction method. In decoding, we use the traditional HPB decoder with CYK and cube pruning.

Figure 3 shows an example of CFRs extraction processing from a pair of word-aligned Japanese-Chinese sentences with a source language CF, and their SCFG style.

3.1 Case Frame Rules Extraction

As described in section 2, the Japanese shallow case frame can be obtained through surface analysis. This way, we can extract case frame reordering rules from sentence pairs with alignment information as shown in Figure 4, where original case

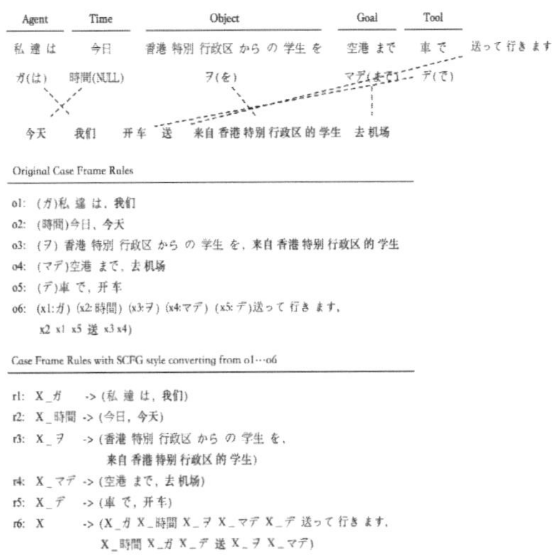

Figure 3: Example of CFRs extraction processing.

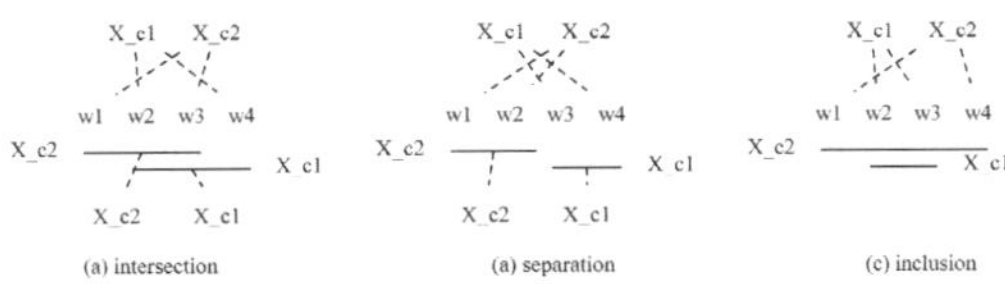

Figure 4: The fuzzy extraction strategy for CF reordering rule.

frame rules are from $o1$ to $o6$.

Given a source language case frame and related word alignment, one case frame is mapped to the case frame reordering rule set,where there are two kinds of rules: reordering rule and phrase rule.

• Phrase rule: Each component in a case frame generates one phrase rule. We extract the phrase rule by following the traditional phrase-based model 's strategy (Och and Ney, 2004). Each phrase rule has a case distinction associated with a shallow case in a case frame like $r1$ to $r5$ in Figure 3.

• Reordering rule: One case frame generates one reordering rule. For reordering rule extraction, we need to compute the relatively order of target language span associated with each case slot. The order is relatively soft to the word alignment. For example, if a source language phrase A covers target span [2, 4] and the other source language phrase B covers target span [1, 3], then the phrase A is relatively right to the phrase B in target side; if a span is covered by the other one, the rule is forbidden during extraction. All of the

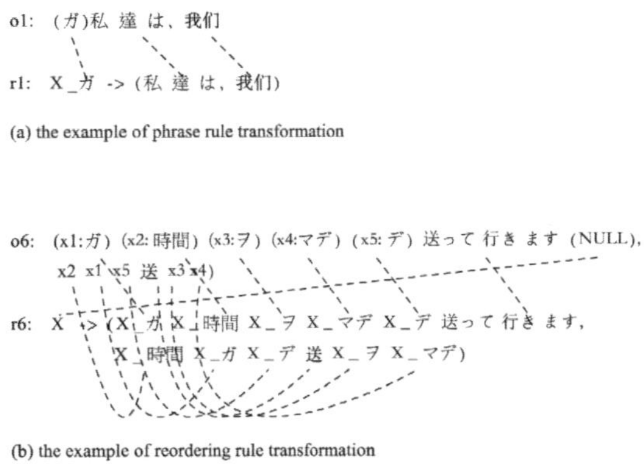

Figure 5: The example of transformation for phrase rule and reordering rule.

possible case frames with word alignment can be seen in Figure 4, where only (c) rule is forbidden. The reordering rule is like $r6$ in Figure 3.

3.2 Transforming Case Frame Rule into SCFG style

To make case frame rules directly accessible to the Hiero-style decoder with performs decoding with SCFG rules, we convert original case frame rules into SCFG style. And then, case frame rule is defined as SCFG-style, which is a little different from hiero rules.

• Phrase rule transformation: We take $o1$ as an example transforming into $r1$ shown in Figure 5(a). We use $o1$'s case distinction as case distinction of $r1$'s left. The source side of the $r1$'s right is source phrase in o1 and the target side is target phrase in $o1$.

• Reordering rules transformation: We take o6 as an example transforming into $r6$ shown in Figure 5(b). We also use $o6$'s verb case distinction as case distinction of $r6$'s left. (default X if there is no case distinction in this example). Each slot of $o6$ is transformed into related X with respective case distinction in $r6$. The target side of the rule 's right is target language 's reordering. It is clearly seen that if there is no non-terminals in the right of reordering rule, reordering rule is the same with phrase rule.

In this way, each case frame rule is associated with exactly one SCFG rule. Therefore, we can obtain a fine-grained SCFG from case frames due to case distinction. On one hand, non-terminals associated with case are linguistically sensible. For example of r4, “空港 まで” with “マデ” case is translated to “去 机场” that means “to airport”. On the other hand, it can capture complex reordering information. For example of r6, the source side of the rule’s right means that “ガ” (who) “時間” (when) “ヲ” (whom) “マデ” (where) “デ” (how) “送って 行き ます” (send)in Japanese order, and the target side of the rule ’s right means that “時間” (when) “ガ” (who) “デ” (how) “送” (send) “デ” (whom) “マデ” (where) in Chinese order.

For reordering the rule extraction, we need to compute the relatively order of target language span associated with each case slot. The order is relatively soft to the word alignment. For example, if a source language phrase A covers target span [2, 4] and the other source language phrase B covers target span [1, 3], then the phrase A is relatively right to the phrase B on the target side; if a span is covered by the other one, the rule is forbidden during extraction. All the possible CFs with word alignment can be seen in Figure 4, where only (c) rule is forbidden.

Generally, we define the transformed case frame rules as SCFG style:

$$X \rightarrow \langle \gamma, \alpha, \sim \rangle \tag{1}$$

Where X is non-terminal, γ and α are both strings of terminals and non-terminals as the same with SCFG in the HPB model. Compared with SCFG in the HPB model, the only difference is that non-terminals are distinguished by case as shown in Figure 3 from $r1$ to $r6$.

3.3 Decoding

Both transformed case frame rules and HPB rules can be applied using traditional Hiero decoders with a slight modification. Here we follow the description of Hiero decoding by Chiang (2007). The source sentence is parsed under the Hiero grammar using the CYK algorithm. Each cell in the CYK grid is associated with a list of rules that applies to its span from the bottom up. For each derivation, we apply cube pruning (Chiang,2007) and beam search technology.

This procedure accommodates traditional HPB rules directly. We use traditional HPB rules for translation as shown in Figure 6(a). For example, the traditional rule can be applied in the span (14,16). Since the span (4, 18) is longer than 10 words, the traditional rule cannot be applied in the span.

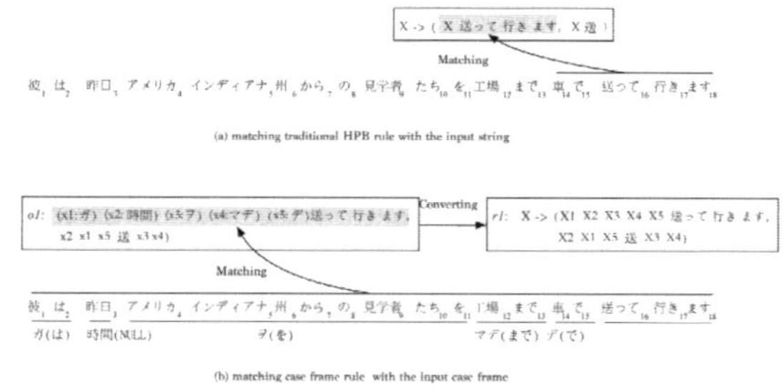

Figure 6: Decoding with both traditional hiero grammar and case frame.

We move our focus towards case frame reordering rules, and analyze sentences and obtain all the case frames, and then for each CF, we match rules to the span related to the CF. If a match is found, the CYK cell for the span is selected, and that rule is added to the list of rules in the selected CYK cell as shown in Figure 6(b). For example, the span (1,18) can be matched with $r6$. The complex reordering can be captured by $r6$.

It is clear that the HPB rules have non-terminals without any distinction and the case frame rules have non-terminals with case distinction. Generally, there are two kinds of non-terminals: X and X with case. During decoding, we respectively use three kinds of constraints on case frame rule matching:

Without constraints ignore all the case distinction in case frame rules, so case frame rule format is the same with HPB rules. In this way, we just expand SCFG.

Soft constraints admit the match between different case distinctions by adding extra dynamic feature – soft count. For example, X with “ヲ” is allowed to match X with “マデ” by adding 1 to soft count.

Hard constraints only admit the completed and exact match. On one hand, we admit X to match all of the X with or without distinction, on the other hand, we only allow X with distinction to match X with the same distinction.

3.4 Features

The baseline feature set used in this work consists of 7 features, including a strong 5-gram language model, bidirectional translation probabilities, bidirectional lexical probabilities, and a word count, a glue rule count. In the CF reordering rule, bidirectional translation probabilities and bidirectional lexical probabilities are also used during decoding. In addition, we introduce several features for applying case frame rules, and we adopt these features to log-linear model during decoding.

• Rule type indicators. For soft or hard constraint, we consider two indicator features, indicating case frame rules, case frame reordering rules. Case frame rules indicator feature is used to distinguish case frame rules and original HPB rules. Case frame reordering rules indicator feature is used to distinguish phrase rules and reordering rules in case frame rule set.

• Dynamic soft constraints. For soft constraints, we consider the soft constraints. Note that when X with case mismatches X with other different case, we add dynamic soft constraints count for this mismatching instead of prohibition.

4 Evaluation

4.1 Experimental Setup

We report results for this Japanese-Chinese task. We use two data sets, where one uses news from the 7th China Workshop on Machine Translation (CWMT) including 280 thousand sentence pairs for training, 500 sentence pairs for parameter optimization and 900 sentence pairs for testing, the other, from Asian Scientific Paper Excerpt Corpus-Japanese to Chinese (ASPEC-JC) includes 680 thousand pairs for training, 2090 sentence pairs for parameter optimization and 1800 sentence pairs for testing.

The source side sentences are parsed by KNP (Kurohashi and Nagao, 1994) into chunk dependency structures whose nodes are at chunk-level. Also we achieve corresponding case frame analysis from byproduct of KNP. The word alignment is obtained by running GIZA++ (Och and Ney, 2003) on the corpus in both direction and applying "grow-diag-and"refinement (Koehn et al., 2003). We apply SRI Language Modeling Toolkit (Stolcke, 2002) to train a 5-gram language model for target side sentences.

4.2 Results

For comparison, we also manually modify the extracted case frame rules of development and test data with case frame information according to the Japanese and Chinese grammar. We report machine translation performance in Table 2 using case insensitive BLEU-4 metric (Papineni et al., 2002), considering the balance of the performance

entry	system	CWMT	
		Rule ♯	BLEU-4
exp1	baseline	14.70M	0.2805
exp2*	exp1 + cfr	14.70M+0.71M	0.2836
manually	exp1 + cfr	/	0.2865
entry	system	ASPEC	
		Rule ♯	BLEU-4
exp1	baseline	215.67M	0.2717
exp2*	exp1 + cfr	215.67+7.21M	0.2748
manually	exp1 + cfr	/	0.2763

Table 2: BLEU[%] scores of various systems. ∗ means that a system is significantly different from the baseline at $p < 0.01$. M means million and $+$ means hierarchical rules with CFRs.

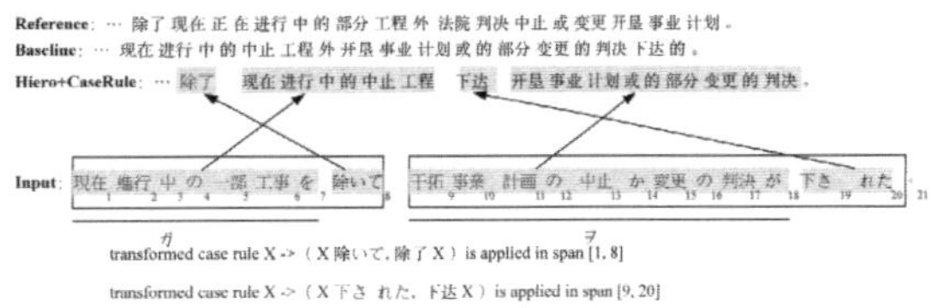

Figure 7: Comparison of translations generated by the baseline and improved systems.

of lexical and phrase. The experiments are organized as follows:

• exp1: we use the NiuTrans (Xiao, 2012) hierarchical phrase-based model as strong baseline system.

• exp2: we transform CFRs into SCFG-style rules without any case distinction, and add these rule into exp1 system.

4.3 Analysis

Finally, we discuss an example of real translation from our test set. See Figure 7 for translations generated from different systems. The Japanese input sentence contains "…下さ れた" which is usually translated into "下达… " (i.e. a transformed CF reordering rule "$X \rightarrow X$ (下さ れた, 下达" X)) . However, because the "…下さ れた" pattern spans 12 words and that is beyond the span limit, our baseline is unable to apply this desired rule and so it chooses the wrong reordering translation. When importing CF reordering rule which captures the CF "（を）下さ れた" , we can transform the CF reordering rule into one that is SCFG-style and achieve right reordering information.

• Better reordering Main structure in Japanese structure is SOV-style, which is different from

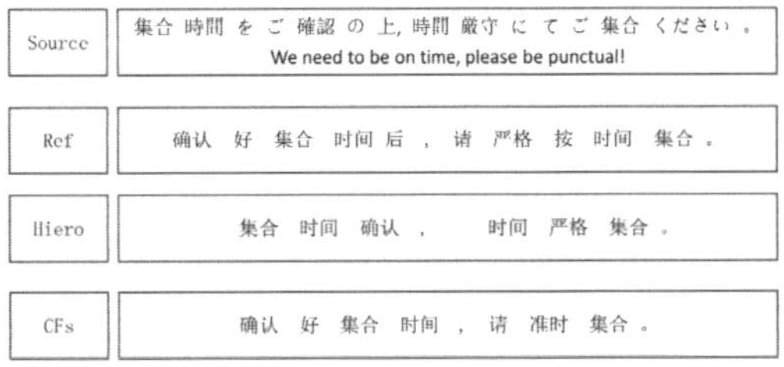

Figure 8: Actual translations produced by the baselines and our system.

Chinese SVO-style. Reordering problem is significant in Japanese- Chinese translation, especially with long phrase for S and/or V. Compared with hierarchical phrase-based rules, case frame rules have better phrase reordering. In the example as shown in Figure 8, the source sentence main centered verbs contain the word "確認(confirm)" and the word "集合(gather)". The Hiero result mistakenly treats that objective phrase as subjective (SOV), thus results in translation with different structure from source sentence. Conversely, our system captures this component relations in case frame and translates it into the SVO structure.

- Better exical translation results Moreover, we also find that our system can get better lexical translation results, for instance, the result of the word "時間厳守(punctuality)",as indicated in Figure 8.

5 Related Work

Recently linguistically-motivated models have been intensively investigated in MT. In particular, source tree-based models (Liu et al., 2006; Huang et al., 2006; Eisner, 2003; Zhang et al., 2008; Liu et al., 2009a; Xie et al., 2011) have received growing interest due to their excellent ability to model source language syntax for better lexical selection and reordering. Alternatively, the hierarchical phrase-based approach (Chiang, 2005) considers the underlying hierarchical structures of sentences but does not require linguistically syntactic trees on either language′s side.

There are several lines of work for augmenting hierarchical phrase-based systems with the use of source language linguistic information. Xiao (2014) incorporates source syntax into the hierarchical phrase-based model. They develop procedures for joint decoding and optimization within a single system by transforming tree-to-string rules into SCFG rules. By enlarging SCFG grammar, they perform well on Chinese-English tasks. Our approach is motivated by high-precision Japanese case analysis, and aims to augment the search space of Hiero with linguistically-motivated hypotheses. Moreover, we consider hiero as the backbone model and only introduce and transform Japanese CF into SCFG rules where they can contribute.

Another related line of work is to introduce pre-ordering approach for Japanese main structure. Wu (2011) and Sudoh (2013) propose several methods to train pre-ordering model for pre-ordering. We note that, we have no need to train extra pre-ordering models for the Japanese main structure, and we only use the high-precision Japanese explicit case analysis to improve Japanese-Chinese translation performance described in this paper.

6 Conclusion and Future Work

We have presented an approach to improving Hiero-style systems by augmenting the SCFG with Japanese case frame rules. The input case frame are used to introduce new linguistically-sensible hypotheses into the translation search space while maintaining the Hiero robustness qualities and avoiding computational explosions. We obtain significant improvements over a strong Hiero baseline in the Japanese-to-Chinese task.

This paper presented an approach to improve HPB model systems by augmenting the SCFG with Japanese CFRs. The CF are used to introduce new linguistically-sensible hypotheses into the translation search space while maintaining the Hiero robustness qualities and avoiding computational explosions. We obtain significant improvements over a strong HPB baseline in the Japanese-to-Chinese task. We will try to improve the performance of our system with soft constraint or hard constraint using case frame rules, and we will challenge to resolve the problem of tense, aspect and some special grammatical sentences of Japanese to Chinese translation.

Acknowledgments

The authors were supported by National Nature Science Foundation of China (Contract 61370130 and 61473294), the Fundamental Research Funds for the Central Universities (2014RC040), and Project 20141004065 supported by National

Training Program of Innovation and Entrepreneurship for Undergraduates.

References

Wu, X., Sudoh, K., Duh, K., Tsukada, H., and Nagata 2011. *Extracting preordering rules from chunk-based dependency trees for Japanese-to-English translation.*, Proceedings of the 13th Machine Translation Summit. pages 300–307.

Chiang, David. 2005. *A hierarchical phrase-based model for statistical machine translation.*,Proceedings of the 43rd Annual Meeting on Association for Computational Linguistics. Association for Computational Linguistics, 2005. pages 263–270.

Chiang, David. 2007. *Hierarchical phrase-based translation.*(J) computational linguistics,33(2),pages 201–228.

Fillmore, C. J. 1967. *The case for case.*

Kiyoshi Y., KAMEI S. and MURAKI K. A. 1997. *A Hybrid Approach to Interactive Machine Translation*,In Proceedings of the Fifteenth International Joint Conference on Artificial Intelligence, Nagoya, Japan, August 23-29, 1997. Morgan Kaufmann, 1997, pages 977–982.

Kawahara, D., and Kurohashi, S. 2002. *Fertilization of case frame dictionary for robust Japanese case analysis.* In Proceedings of the 19th international conference on Computational linguistics-Volume 1, 2002, pages 1–7, Association for Computational Linguistics.

Kawahara D, Kurohashi S. 2006. *Case frame compilation from the web using high-performance computing.* In Proceedings of the 5th International Conference on Language Resources and Evaluation. 2006, pages 1344–1347.

Och F. J. and Ney H. 2004. *TextRank: The alignment template approach to statistical machine translation[J]*, Computational linguistics, 2004, 30(4): 417–449.

Hajič J., Ciaramita M., Johansson R.,et al. 2009. *shared task: Syntactic and semantic dependencies in multiple languages.* In Proceedings of the Thirteenth Conference on Computational Natural Language Learning: Shared Task. Association for Computational Linguistics, 2009, pages 1–18.

Liu Y, Liu Q, Lin S. 2006. *Tree-to-string alignment template for statistical machine translation*, In Proceedings of the 21st International Conference on Computational Linguistics and the 44th annual meeting of the Association for Computational Linguistics. Association for Computational Linguistics, 2006, pages 609–616.

Huang, L., Knight, K. and Joshi, A. 2006. *Statistical syntax-directed translation with extended domain of locality.* In Proceedings of AMTA pages 66–73.

Eisner J. 2003. *Learning non-isomorphic tree mappings for machine translation.* In Proceedings of the 41st Annual Meeting on Association for Computational Linguistics-Volume 2. Association for Computational Linguistics, 2003, pages, 205–208.

Min Zhang,Hongfei Jiang,Haizhou Li,Chew Lim Tan and Sheng Li. 2008. *A tree sequence alignment-based tree-to-tree translation model.* In Proceedings of ACL-08: HLT (2008): 559.

Liu Y, Lü Y, Liu Q. 2009. *Improving tree-to-tree translation with packed forests.* In Proceedings of the Joint Conference of the 47th Annual Meeting of the ACL and the 4th International Joint Conference on Natural Language Processing of the AFNLP: Volume 2-Volume 2. Association for Computational Linguistics, 2009, pages 558–566.

Xie J., Mi H. and Liu Q. 2011. *A novel dependency-to-string model for statistical machine translation*, In Proceedings of the Conference on Empirical Methods in Natural Language Processing. Association for Computational Linguistics, 2011, pages 216-226.

Xiao, T., Zhu, J., Zhang, H. and Li, Q. 2012. *NiuTrans: an open source toolkit for phrase-based and syntax-based machine translation*,In Proceedings of the ACL 2012 System Demonstrations. Association for Computational Linguistics, pages 19–24.

Tong Xiao, Adrià de Gispert, Jingbo Zhu and Bill Byrne. 2014. *Effective Incorporation of Source Syntax into Hierarchical Phrase-based Translation.* In Proceedings of Coling 2014, pages 2064-2074.

Sudoh K, Wu X, Duh K, et al. 2013. *Syntax-Based Post-Ordering for Efficient Japanese-to-English Translation.* ACM Transactions on Asian Language Information Processing (TALIP), 2013, 12(3): 12.

A Discriminative Model for Semantics-to-String Translation

Aleš Tamchyna
Charles University in Prague
Malostranské náměstí 25
Prague, Czech Republic
tamchyna@ufal.mff.cuni.cz

Chris Quirk and **Michel Galley**
Mircosoft Research
One Microsoft Way
Redmond, WA 98052
{chrisq,mgalley}@microsoft.com

Abstract

We present a feature-rich discriminative model for machine translation which uses an abstract semantic representation on the source side. We include our model as an additional feature in a phrase-based decoder and we show modest gains in BLEU score in an n-best re-ranking experiment.

1 Introduction

The goal of machine translation is to take source language utterances and convert them into fluent target language utterances with the same meaning. Most recent approaches learn transformations using statistical techniques on parallel data. Meaning equivalent representations of words and phrases are learned directly from natural data, as are other syntactic operations such as reordering. However, commonly used methods have a very simple view of the linguistic data. Each word is generally modeled independently, for instance, and the relations between words are generally captured only in fixed phrases or as syntactic relationships.

Recently there has been a resurgence of interest in unified semantic representations: deep analyses with heavy normalization of morphology, syntax, and even semantic representations. In particular, *Abstract Meaning Representation* (AMR, Banarescu et al. (2013)) is a novel representation of (sentential) semantics. Such representations could influence a number of natural language understanding and generation tasks, particularly machine translation.

Deeper models can be used for multiple aspects of the translation modeling problem. Building translation models that rely on a deeper representation of the input allows for a more parsimonious translation model: morphologically related words can be handled in a unified manner; semantically related concepts are immediately adjacent and available for modeling, etc. Language models using deep representations might help us model which interpretations are more plausible.

We present an initial discriminative method for modeling the likelihood of a target language surface string given source language deep semantics. This approach relies on an automatic parser for source language semantics. We use a system that parses into AMR-like structures (Vanderwende et al., 2015), and apply the resulting model as an additional feature in a translation system.

2 Related Work

There is a large body of related work on utilizing deep language representation in NLP and MT in particular. This is not surprising considering that such representations provide abstractions of many language-specific phenomena, effectively bringing different languages closer together.

A number of machine translation systems starting as early as the 1950s therefore used a form of transfer: the source sentences were parsed, and those parsed representations were translated into target representations. Finally text generation was applied. The level of analysis is somewhat arguable – sometimes it was purely syntactic, but in other cases it reached into the semantic domain.

One of the earliest architectures was described in 1957 (Yngve, 1957). More contemporary examples of such systems include KANT (Nyberg and Mitamura, 1992), which used a very deep representation close to an interlingua, early versions of SysTran and Microsoft Translator, or more recently TectoMT (Popel and Žabokrtský, 2010) for English→Czech translation.

AMR itself has recently been used for abstractive summarization (Liu et al., 2015). In this work, sentences in the document to be summarized are parsed to AMRs, then a decoding algorithm is run to produce a summary graph. The surface realization of this graph then constitutes the final sum-

Proceedings of the 1st Workshop on Semantics-Driven Statistical Machine Translation, pages 30–36,
Beijing, China, July 30, 2015.

```
like1 (+Futr +Proposition +T3 +SubC +Probabl +WeakOblig)
 Dsub——I1 (+Pers1 +Sing +Anim +Humn)
 Dobj——give1 (+D1 +T1 +Loc_sr)
        Dsub——I1
        Dind——you1 (+Pers2 +Sing +Plur +Anim +Humn)
        Dobj——sandwich1 (+Indef +Pers3 +Sing +Conc +Count +Food)
                Attrib—take1 (+Pass +Proposition +T1 +ECM +Loc_sr)
                        Dsub——_X1
                        Dobj——sandwich1
                        Source—fridge1 (+Def +Pers3 +Sing +Conc +Count)
```

Figure 1: Logical Form (computed tree) for the sentence: *I would like to give you a sandwich taken from the fridge.*

mary.

(Jones et al., 2012) presents an MT approach that can exploit semantic graphs such as AMR, in a continuation of earlier work that abstracted translation away from strings (Yamada and Knight, 2001; Galley et al., 2004). While rule extraction algorithms such as (Galley et al., 2004) operate on trees and have also been applied to semantic parsing problems (Li et al., 2013), Jones et al. (2012) generalized these approaches by inducing synchronous hyperedge replacement grammars (HRG), which operate on graphs. In contrast to (Jones et al., 2012), our work does not have to deal with the complexities of HRG decoding, which runs in $O(n^3)$ (Jones et al., 2012), as our decoder is simply a phrase-based decoder.

Discriminative models have been used in statistical MT many times. Global lexicon model (Mauser et al., 2009) and phrase-sense disambiguation (Carpuat and Wu, 2007) are perhaps the best known methods. Similarly to Carpuat and Wu (2007), we use the classifier to rescore phrasal translations, however we do not train a separate classifier for each source phrase. Instead, we train a global model – similarly to Subotin (2011) or more recently Tamchyna et al. (2014). Features for our model are very different from previous work because they come from a deep representation and therefore should capture semantic relations between the languages, instead of surface or morpho-syntactic correspondences.

3 Semantic Representation

Our representation of sentence semantics is based on Logical Form (Vanderwende, 2015). LFs are labeled directed graphs whose nodes roughly correspond to content words in the sentence. Edge labels describe semantic relations between nodes. Additional linguistic information, such as verb subcategorization frames, definiteness, tense etc., is stored in graph nodes as *bits*.

Figure 1 shows a sentence parsed into the logical form. Nodes are represented by word lemmas. Relations include *Dsub* for deep subject, *Dobj* and *Dind* for direct and indirect objects etc. Bits are shown as flags in parentheses. Note that this graph may have cycles – for example, the *Dobj* of "take" is "sandwich", but "take" is also the *Attrib* of "sandwich". The verb "take" is also missing its obligatory subject which is replaced by the free variable *_X*.

The logical form can be converted using a sequence of rules to a representation which conforms to the AMR specification (Vanderwende et al., 2015). We do not use the full conversion pipeline in our work, so our semantic graphs are somewhere between the LF and AMR. Notably, we keep the *bits* which serve as important features for the discriminative modeling of translation.

4 Graph-to-String Translation

We develop models for semantic-graph-to-string translation. These models are essentially discriminative translation models, relying on a decomposition structure similar to both maximum entropy language models and IBM Models 1, 2 (Brown et al., 1993), and the HMM translation model (Vogel et al., 1996). In particular, we see translation as a process of selecting target words in order conditioned on source language representation as well as prior target words. Similar to the IBM Models, we see each target word as being generated based on source concepts, though in our case the concepts are semantic graph nodes rather than surface words. That is, we assume the existence of an alignment, though it aligns the target words to

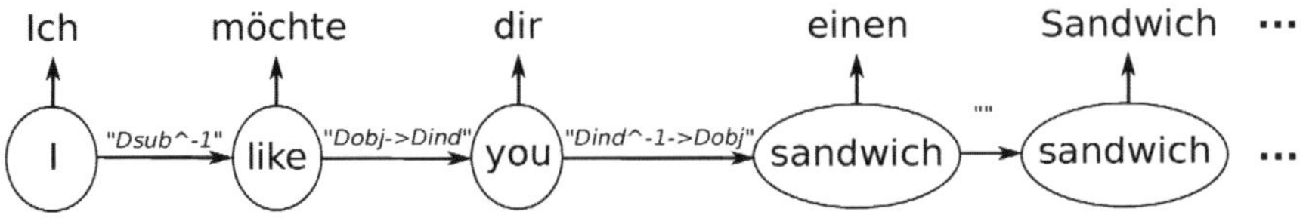

Figure 2: An example of the translation process illustrating several first steps of translating the sentence from Figure 1 into German (*"Ich möchte dir einen Sandwich..."*). Labels in italics correspond to the shortest undirected paths between the nodes.

source semantic graph nodes rather than surface words.

Our model views translation as generation of the target-side sentence given the source-side semantic graph. We assume a generative process which operates as follows. We begin in the virtual root node of the graph. At each step, we transition to a graph node and we generate a target-side word. We proceed left-to-right on the target side and we stop once the whole target sentence is generated. Figure 2 shows an example of this process.

Say we have a source semantic graph G with nodes $V = \{n_1..n_S\}$, edges $E \subset V \times V$, and a root node n_R for $R \in 1..S$. Then the likelihood of a target string $E = (e_1, ..., e_T)$ and alignment $A = (a_1, ..., a_T)$ with $a_i \in 0..S$ is as follows, with $a_0 = R$:

$$P(A, E|G) = \prod_{i=1}^{T} P(a_i|a_1^{i-1}, e_1^{i-1}, G) \\ P(e_i|a_1^{i}, e_1^{i-1}, G) \quad (1)$$

In this generative story, we first predict each alignment position and then predict each translated word. The transition distribution $P(a_i|\cdots)$ resembles that of the HMM alignment model, though the features are somewhat different. The translation distribution $P(e_i|\cdots)$ may take on several forms. For the purposes of alignment, we explore a simple categorical distribution as in the IBM models. For translation reranking, we instead use a feature-rich approach conditioned on a variety of source and target context.

4.1 Alignment of Semantic Graph Nodes

We have experimented with a number of techniques for aligning source-side semantic graph nodes to target-side surface words.

Gibbs sampling. We can attempt to directly align the target language words to the source language nodes using a generative HMM-style model. Unlike the HMM word alignment model (Vogel et al., 1996), the likelihood of jumping between nodes is based on the graph path between those nodes, rather than the linear distance.

Starting from the generative story of Equation 1, we make several simplifying assumptions. First we assume that the alignment distribution $P(a_i|\cdots)$ is modeled as a categorical distribution:

$$P(a_i|a_{i-1}, G) \propto \mathrm{c}(\text{LABEL}(a_{i-1}, a_i))$$

The function LABEL*(u, v)* produces a string describing the labels along the shortest (undirected) path between the two nodes.

Next, we assume that the translation distribution is modeled as a set of categorical distributions, one for each source semantic node:

$$P(e_i|n_{a_i}) \propto \mathrm{c}(\text{LEMMA}(n_{a_i}) \rightarrow e_i)$$

This model is sensitive to the order in which source language information is presented in the target language.

The alignment variables a_i are not observed. We use Gibbs sampling rather than EM so that we can incorporate a sparse prior when estimating the parameters of the model and the assignments to these latent alignment variables. At each iteration, we shuffle the sentences in our training data. Then for each sentence, we visit all its tokens in a random order and re-align them. We sample the new alignment according to the Markov blanket, which has the following probability distribution:

$$P(t|n_i) \propto \frac{\mathrm{c}(\text{LEMMA}(n_i) \rightarrow t) + \alpha}{\mathrm{c}(\text{LEMMA}(n_i)) + \alpha L} \times \frac{\mathrm{c}(\text{LABEL}(n_i, n_{i-1})) + \beta}{T + \beta P} \times \frac{\mathrm{c}(\text{LABEL}(n_{i+1}, n_i)) + \beta}{T + \beta P} \quad (2)$$

L, P stand for the number of lemma/path *types*, respectively. T is the total number of tokens in the corpus. Overall, the formula describes the probability of the edge coming into the node n_i, the token emission and finally the outgoing edge. We evaluate this probability for each node n_i in the graph and re-align the token according to the random sample from this distribution.

α and β are hyper-parameters specifying the concentration parameters of symmetric Dirichlet priors over the transition and emission distributions. Specifying values less than 1 for these hyper-parameters pushes the model toward sparse solutions. They are tuned by a grid search which evaluates model perplexity on a held-out set.

Direct GIZA++. GIZA++ (Och and Ney, 2000) is a commonly used toolkit for word alignment which implements the IBM models. In this setting, we linearized the semantic graph nodes using a simple heuristic based on the surface word order and aligned them directly to the target-side sentences. We experimented with different symmetrizations and found that grow-diag-final-and gives the best results.

Composed alignments. We divided the alignment problem into two stages: aligning semantic graph nodes to source-side words and aligning the source- and target-side words (i.e., standard MT word alignment). We then simply compose the two alignments. For the alignment between source graph nodes and source surface words, we have two options: we can either train a GIZA++ model or we can use gold alignments provided by the semantic parser. For the second stage, we need to train a GIZA++ model.

We evaluated the different strategies by manually inspecting the resulting alignments. We found that the composition of two separate alignment steps produces clearly superior results, even if it seems arguable whether such division simplifies the task. Therefore, for the remaining experiments, we used the composition of gold alignment and GIZA++, although two GIZA++ steps performed comparably well.

4.2 Model

For our discriminative model, the alignment is assumed to be given. At training time, it is the alignment produced by the parser composed with GIZA++ surface word alignment. At test time, we compose the alignment between graph nodes and source surface tokens (given by the parser) with the bilingual surface word alignment provided by the MT decoder.

Turning to the translation distribution, we use a maximum entropy model to learn the conditional probability:

$$P(e_i|n_{a_i}, n_{a_{i-1}}, G, e_{i-k+1}^{i-1}) = \frac{\exp\left(\mathbf{w} \cdot \mathbf{f}(e_i, n_{a_i}, n_{a_{i-1}}, G, e_{i-k+1}^{i-1})\right)}{Z} \quad (3)$$

where Z is defined as

$$\sum_{e' \in GEN(n_{a_i})} \exp(\mathbf{w} \cdot \mathbf{f}(e', n_{a_i}, n_{a_{i-1}}, G, e_{i-k+1}^{i-1}))$$

The *GEN(n)* function produces the possible translations of the deep lemma associated with node n. We collect all translations observed in the training data and keep the 30 most frequent ones for each lemma. Our model thus assigns zero probability to unseen translations.

Because of the size of our training data, we used online learning. We implemented a parallelized (multi-threaded) version of the standard stochastic gradient descent algorithm (SGD). Our learning rate was fixed – using line search, we found the optimal rate to be 0.05. Our batch size was set to one; different batch sizes made almost no difference in model performance. We used online L1 regularization (Tsuruoka et al., 2009) with weight 1. We implemented feature hashing to further improve performance and set the hash length to 22 bits. We shuffled our data and split it into five parts which were processed independently and their final weights were averaged.

4.3 Feature Set

Our semantic representation enables us to use a very rich set of features, including information commonly used by both translation models and language models. We extract a significant amount of information from the graph node n_{a_i} aligned to the generated word:

- lemma,
- part of speech,
- all bits.

We extract the same features from the previous graph node ($n_{a_{i-1}}$), from the parent node. (If there are multiple parents in the graph, we break ties in a consistent but heuristic manner, picking the left-most parent node according to its position in the source sentence) We also gather all the bits of the parent and the parent relation. These features may capture agreement phenomena.

We also look at the shortest path in the semantic graph from the previous node to the current one and we extract features which describe it:

- path length,
- relations (edges) along the path.

We use the lemmas of all nodes in the semantic graph as bag-of-word features, as well as all the surface words in the source sentence. We also extract lemmas of nodes within a given distance from the current node (i.e. graph context), as well as the relation that led to these nodes. Together, these features ground the current node in its semantic context.

An additional set of features handle the fact that source nodes may generate multiple target words, and the distribution over subsequent words should be different. We have a feature indicating the number of words generated from the current node, both in isolation, conjoined with the lemma, and conjoined with the part of speech. We also have a feature for each word previously generated by this same node, again in isolation, in conjunction with the lemma, and in conjunction with the part of speech. This helps prevent the model from generating multiple copies of same target word given a source node.

On the target side, we use several previous tokens as features. These may act as discriminative language model features.

During MT decoding, our model therefore must maintain state, which could present a computational issue. The language model features present similar complexity as conventional MT state, and the features about prior words generated from the same node require greater memory. Were this cost to become prohibitive, a simpler form of the prior word features would likely suffice.

5 Experiments

We tested our model in an n-best re-ranking experiment.

We began by training a basic phrase-based MT system for English→French on 1 million parallel sentence pairs and produced 1000-best lists for three test sets provided for the Workshop on Statistical Machine Translation (Bojar et al., 2013) – WMT 2009, 2010 and 2013. This system had a set of 13 commonly used features: four channel model scores (forward and backward MLE and lexical weighting scores), a 5-gram language model, five lexicalized reordering model scores (corresponding to different ordering outcomes), linear distortion penalty, word count, and phrase count. The system was optimized using minimum error rate training (Och, 2003) on WMT 2009.

Dataset	Baseline	+Semantics
WMT 2009 = devset	17.44	17.55
WMT 2010	17.59	17.64
WMT 2013	17.41	17.55

Table 1: BLEU scores of n-best reranking in English→French translation.

For reranking, we gathered 1000-best lists for the development and test sets. We added six scores from our model to each translation in the n-best lists. We included the total log probability, the sum of unnormalized scores, and the rank of the given output. In addition, we had count features indicating the number of words that were not in the GEN set of the model, the number of NULLs (effectively deleted nodes), and a count of times a target word appeared in a stopword list. In the end, each translation had a total of 19 features: 13 from the original features and 6 from this approach.

Next, we ran one iteration of the MERT optimizer on these 1000-best lists for all of the features. Because this was a reranking experiment rather than decoding, we did not repeatedly gather n-best lists as in decoding. The resulting feature weights were used to rescore the test n-best lists and evaluated the using BLEU; Table 1 shows the results. We obtained a modest but consistent improvement. Once the model is used directly in the decoder, the gains should increase as it will be able to influence decoding.

6 Conclusion

We have presented an initial attempt at including semantic features in a statistical machine translation system. Our approach uses discriminative training and a broad set of features to capture morphological, syntactic, and semantic information in a single model. Although our gains are not particularly large yet, we believe that additional effort on feature engineering and decoder integration could lead to more substantial gains.

Our approach is gated by the accuracy and consistency of the semantic parser. We have used a broad coverage parser with accuracy competitive to the current state-of-the-art, but even the state-of-the-art is rather low. It would be interesting to explore more robust features spanning multiple analyses, or to combine the outputs of multiple parsers. Even syntax-based machine translation systems are dependent on accurate parsers (Quirk and Corston-Oliver, 2006); deeper analyses are likely to be more dependent on parse quality.

In a similar vein, it would be interesting to evaluate the impact of morphological, syntactic, and semantic features separately. A careful feature ablation and exploration would help identify promising areas for future research.

We have only scratched the surface of possible integrations. Even this model could be applied to MT systems in multiple ways. For instance, rather than applying from source to target, we might evaluate in a noisy channel sense. That is, we could predict the source language surface forms given the target language translations. Furthermore, this would allow incorporation of a target semantic language model. This latter approach is particularly attractive, as it would explicitly model the semantic plausibility of the target. Of course, this would require target language semantic analysis: either we would be forced to parse n-best outcomes from some baseline system, or integrate the construction of target language semantics into the MT system. We believe that including such models of semantic plausibility holds great promise in preventing "word salad" outputs from MT systems: sentences that simply cannot be interpreted by humans.

Acknowledgements

We would like to thank Lucy Vanderwende and Arul Menezes for their helpful suggestions and insights into the logical form and abstract representations of meaning in general.

References

Laura Banarescu, Claire Bonial, Shu Cai, Madalina Georgescu, Kira Griffitt, Ulf Hermjakob, Kevin Knight, Philipp Koehn, Martha Palmer, and Nathan Schneider. 2013. Abstract meaning representation for sembanking. In *Proceedings of the 7th Linguistic Annotation Workshop and Interoperability with Discourse*, pages 178–186, Sofia, Bulgaria, August. Association for Computational Linguistics.

Ondřej Bojar, Christian Buck, Chris Callison-Burch, Christian Federmann, Barry Haddow, Philipp Koehn, Christof Monz, Matt Post, Radu Soricut, and Lucia Specia. 2013. Findings of the 2013 Workshop on Statistical Machine Translation. In *Eighth Workshop on Statistical Machine Translation*, WMT, pages 1–44, Sofia, Bulgaria.

Peter F Brown, Vincent J Della Pietra, Stephen A Della Pietra, and Robert L Mercer. 1993. The mathematics of statistical machine translation: Parameter estimation. *Computational linguistics*, 19(2):263–311.

Marine Carpuat and Dekai Wu. 2007. Improving Statistical Machine Translation using Word Sense Disambiguation. Prague, Czech Republic.

Michel Galley, Mark Hopkins, Kevin Knight, and Daniel Marcu. 2004. What's in a translation rule? In *Proc. of HLT-NAACL*, pages 273–280.

Bevan Jones, Jacob Andreas, Daniel Bauer, Karl Moritz Hermann, and Kevin Knight. 2012. Semantics-based machine translation with hyperedge replacement grammars. In *Proc. of COLING*, pages 1359–1376.

Peng Li, Yang Liu, and Maosong Sun. 2013. An extended ghkm algorithm for inducing lambda-scfg. In *Proc. of AAAI*.

Fei Liu, Jeffrey Flanigan, Sam Thomson, Norman Sadeh, and Noah A. Smith. 2015. Toward abstractive summarization using semantic representations. In *Proceedings of NAACL 2015*, Denver, Colorado, June. Association for Computational Linguistics.

Arne Mauser, Sasa Hasan, and Hermann Ney. 2009. Extending Statistical Machine Translation with Discriminative and Trigger-Based Lexicon Models. pages 210–218, Suntec, Singapore.

Eric H. Nyberg and Teruko Mitamura. 1992. The kant system: Fast, accurate, high-quality translation in practical domains. In *Proceedings of the 14th Conference on Computational Linguistics - Volume 3*, COLING '92, pages 1069–1073, Stroudsburg, PA, USA. Association for Computational Linguistics.

Franz Josef Och and Hermann Ney. 2000. Improved Statistical Alignment Models. In *Proc. of ACL*, pages 440–447, Hong Kong. ACL.

Franz Josef Och. 2003. Minimum Error Rate Training in Statistical Machine Translation. In *Proc. of the Association for Computational Linguistics*, Sapporo, Japan, July 6-7.

Martin Popel and Zdeněk Žabokrtský. 2010. TectoMT: Modular NLP Framework. In Hrafn Loftsson, Eirikur Rögnvaldsson, and Sigrun Helgadottir, editors, *IceTAL 2010*, volume 6233 of *LNCS*, pages

293–304. Iceland Centre for Language Technology (ICLT), Springer.

Chris Quirk and Simon Corston-Oliver. 2006. The impact of parse quality on syntactically-informed statistical machine translation. In *Proceedings of the 2006 Conference on Empirical Methods in Natural Language Processing*, pages 62–69, Sydney, Australia, July. Association for Computational Linguistics.

Michael Subotin. 2011. An exponential translation model for target language morphology. In *Proceedings of the 49th Annual Meeting of the Association for Computational Linguistics: Human Language Technologies - Volume 1*, HLT '11, pages 230–238, Stroudsburg, PA, USA. Association for Computational Linguistics.

Aleš Tamchyna, Fabienne Braune, Alexander Fraser, Marine Carpuat, Hal Daumé III, and Chris Quirk. 2014. Integrating a discriminative classifier into phrase-based and hierarchical decoding. In *The Prague Bulletin of Mathematical Linguistics*.

Yoshimasa Tsuruoka, Jun'ichi Tsujii, and Sophia Ananiadou. 2009. Stochastic gradient descent training for l1-regularized log-linear models with cumulative penalty. In *Proceedings of the Joint Conference of the 47th Annual Meeting of the ACL and the 4th International Joint Conference on Natural Language Processing of the AFNLP: Volume 1-Volume 1*, pages 477–485. Association for Computational Linguistics.

Lucy Vanderwende, Arul Menezes, and Chris Quirk. 2015. An AMR parser for English, French, German, Spanish and Japanese and new AMR-annotated corpus. In *Proceedings of the 2015 NAACL HLT Demonstration Session*, Denver, Colorado, June. Association for Computational Linguistics.

Lucy Vanderwende. 2015. Nlpwin – an introduction. Technical Report MSR-TR-2015-23, March.

Stephan Vogel, Hermann Ney, and Christoph Tillmann. 1996. Hmm-based word alignment in statistical translation. In *Proceedings of the 16th Conference on Computational Linguistics - Volume 2*, COLING '96, pages 836–841, Stroudsburg, PA, USA. Association for Computational Linguistics.

Kenji Yamada and Kevin Knight. 2001. A syntax-based statistical translation model. In *Proc. of ACL*, pages 523–530.

V. H. Yngve. 1957. A framework for syntactic translation. *Mechanical Translation*, 4(3):59–65.

Author Index